Advance Praise
for *The EQ Intervention*

"In *The EQ Intervention*, school psychologist Adam Saenz offers teachers practical Social and Emotional Learning Skills that will help them maintain effective relationships with every student, every day."

—Todd Whitaker, Ph.D.; Distinguished Adjunct Professor, College of Education, University of Missouri; author of *What Great Teachers Do Differently*

"Dr. Saenz's experience working with students and staff makes this book a very powerful tool for all educators. This book validates how social and emotional learning impacts school cultures and positively impacts academics in the process. Emotional intelligence is an essential component of education—of life!"

—Orlando Farias, principal, Mission Collegiate High School, Mission Consolidated School District

"Kudos to Dr. Adam Saenz for laying the groundwork for best practices in Social and Emotional Learning! As educators, we often focus our work on improving instruction in order to meet standardized testing expectations but fall short in addressing this critical area. Now more than ever, we must provide social and emotional learning as statistics continue to show that mental health concerns are clearly on the rise in our younger children. *The EQ Intervention* goes beyond school safety and emphasizes why we must prepare our youth to handle the adversities of life. Simply put, our children's lives depend on social emotional learning. Thank you, Adam, for always being a 'Life Giver.' Your insight and kindness never cease to amaze me."

—Diana Otero, Ph.D., Director of Special Services,
Ysleta Independent School District

"*The EQ Intervention* is not just about how to improve the social and emotional learning that occurs in our classrooms. It is more than a book about identifying ways for educators to work with students so they find a place of belonging and investment in school. It is a book about connecting: connecting with ourselves (within the walls of our own hearts and minds) and connecting with each other (within the walls of our homes and within the streets of our neighborhoods). It brings insight, wisdom and compelling arguments to the necessity of having smart hearts to make our schools and (in my opinion), our homes and communities more connected and safer for everyone."

—James Deegear, Ph.D., L.S.S.P., A.B.P.P., Associate Director,
Student Counseling Services, Texas A&M University

"A valuable, extensively researched guide for helping support educators. Students will learn the SEL competencies they will need for maximizing their opportunity to live successful and fulfilling lives."

—Harvey Deutschendorf, author of *The Other Kind of Smart, Simple Ways to Boost Your Emotional Intelligence for Greater Personal Effectiveness and Success*

"Dr. Saenz uses humor and wit, along with personalized stories, to make the intimidating topic of EQ and SEL understandable and even intriguing. The real life examples and applications presented are eye-opening and invoke self-reflection. If The Power of a Teacher impacted classroom educators, *The EQ Intervention* will impact educational leadership."

—Magan Martin, Coffeyville Public Schools Board Member and Parent Educator with a National Early Childhood Home Visitation Program

THE

EQ

Intervention

ADAM L. SAENZ, PhD

THE
EQ
Intervention

Shaping a Self-Aware Generation
Through Social and Emotional Learning

RIVER GROVE
BOOKS

Published by River Grove Books
Austin, TX
www.rivergrovebooks.com

Distributed by River Grove Books

Design and composition by Greenleaf Book Group
Cover design by Greenleaf Book Group
Cover and interior images: ©shutterstock.com/Martial Red;
©shutterstock.com/Lyudmyla Kharlamova

Publisher's Cataloging-in-Publication data is available.

Print ISBN: 978-1-63299-441-7

eBook ISBN: 978-1-62634-679-6

First Edition

Educating the mind without educating the heart is no education at all.

—Aristotle, philosopher

CONTENTS

Introduction 1

CHAPTER 1
Why Social and Emotional Learning? 17

CHAPTER 2
How Can We Know Ourselves? 57

CHAPTER 3
How Can We Regulate Ourselves? 87

CHAPTER 4
How Can We Know Others? 121

CHAPTER 5
How Can We Engage With Others? 145

CHAPTER 6
What Is the EQ-uipped Classroom? 167

CHAPTER 7
Conclusion: If It Is to Be, It Is Up to Me 193

Appendix: The EASEL Sample Report 211

Index 239

Acknowledgments 247

About the Author 251

Introduction

My Journey Into SEL

To be honest, when I started researching SEL (Social and Emotional Learning) in 2005, I wasn't aware of its long-reaching benefits; I came to it as many in education do, in search of solutions to the problem of school violence. It wasn't until our clinical and research teams sat down to write the EQ-uipped Classroom curriculum that the light bulb of SEL's power illuminated for me. The idea for the curriculum was conceived thirteen years ago in the saltwater bays of Port Mansfield, Texas.

Mike Garcia loves to fish as much as anyone I know, and he's good at it, too. I met Mike the summer before we started second grade, and we've fished together since. It was Labor Day weekend of 2005—opening day of dove season—and the saltwater flats were still producing nice stringers of speckled trout.

Mike and I walked slowly, side-by-side, through knee-high water, wade-fishing through the same bay we had fished in as second graders. It was still early afternoon, and we were keenly aware of the quiet, hot stillness that comes before the evening bite.

"How's the security industry?" I asked as we moved toward a cove, hoping to scare up a redfish in the meantime. Mike entered the security industry right out of college, selling hard and soft systems to the government. In something of a mid-life career shift, he made school districts his clients and never looked back.

"Booming," he said, without missing a beat. "You know, it's kind of sad in a way. Seems like ever since Columbine, we haven't been able to keep up with the demand for greater security in schools. Doors, locks, cameras, metal detectors, you name it."

"How about you?" he asked. "How are things on the mental health end of things?"

"Like you said," I responded wistfully, "kind of sad in a way. We're seeing more and more psychopathology at younger ages. I'm talking about the *little* kids—preschoolers coming to school with symptoms of depression and anxiety. And it's not just that these are spoiled kids with no parenting. There are family issues sometimes, sure, but it just seems like kids are facing a world that we never faced." In our day, Mike and I had faced our fair share of violence; looking back, I believe so much tragedy we experienced could have been avoided if we'd had access to adults who could have instructed us in how to manage our feelings. Partly because of this lack of guidance, not all of our friends made it to adulthood.

"So, do you think that's what all this gun violence is about?" he asked. "Do you think these kids just have mental illness that isn't being treated?"

I paused. "Honestly, I don't think so. I mean, I certainly don't think that's all there is to it. In fact, most kids that commit acts of violence have no diagnosable psychopathology."

"It just seems like we ought to be providing some kind of mental health services for kids," he said with a tone of dissatisfaction in his voice. "I don't know, maybe something that can actually prevent violence from the inside out."

"Absolutely," I agreed. "We're apparently okay with turning our schools into fortresses, and I guess maybe that's needed, but no one seems to be realizing that heart smarts is the ghost in the school safety machine."

"Heart smarts?" he asked, not quite following.

"Yeah. You know—we talk about a person having book smarts, meaning they can learn quickly and do well in school, and we know there are certain benefits associated with that. And we talk about a person having street smarts, and you and I both know the benefits associated with that." He chuckled. "But it's really heart smarts that pay off in the long run. Just knowing how to manage yourself and relate with other people. I mean think about it: With college degrees becoming more and more common, it's heart smarts that are making candidates more desirable to employers."

"Heart smarts," he repeated with a sense of reflection. "I like it. You should write a book."

I didn't know if he said that because he really meant it, or if he was just being nice because he already had three trout on his stringer to my zero. Either way, I didn't write a book. What I did do was create a rough outline for a curriculum. I started by conducting a review of literature on the effectiveness of interventions that targeted bullying, and that led me into the broader arena of SEL. What if we could teach students to recognize and manage their emotions in age-appropriate ways? What if we could teach students empathy and effective conflict resolution? And what if we had teachers and administrators on campuses that purposely modeled those skills? Surely that would represent an inside-out approach to school safety.

I went back to Mike with an executive summary of that initial curriculum. He loved it, and we had the idea to offer it to school districts in conjunction with security systems: Instead of just depending on technology to keep kids safe, what if we empowered them—and adults—with a relevant skill set that would not only keep them safe, but ultimately improve the school's overall climate?

When we presented the idea to district leaders, they seemed confused, clearly not making the connection between aggression and the lack of prosocial training. Looking back, I'm not quite sure what they heard *("... And by the way, we can offer you those locks and cameras and metal detectors bundled with a supply of mood rings and school-wide banjo lessons")*. Keep in mind, while this was six years post-Columbine, it was still before the shootings in Red Lake, Blacksburg, Newtown, Parkland, and Santa Fe. The broader sense of urgency about SEL and the understanding of its relevance hadn't yet matured.

I was discouraged, and I put down my research on SEL. As I continued to work in schools, I started seeing more and more teachers experience burnout, so I wrote *The Power of a Teacher*, a book about self-care. Then, as more and more educators began to realize the link between learning and relationships, I wrote *Relationships That Work*, a book about the four must-have skills for building effective relationships.

Meanwhile, Red Lake. Then Blacksburg. Then Newtown. Then Parkland. Then, 130 miles from my children's school, Santa Fe.

Thirteen years after that fishing trip with Mike, with renewed vigor, I circled back to SEL research and that initial draft of the yet-to-be-named curriculum. Only recently—maybe in the last six months—have I begun to appreciate how all-encompassing the potential benefits of SEL skills really are.

Since we know that emotional intelligence can be measured, our clinical team at the Oakwood Collaborative partnered with Dr. Myeongsun Yoon—an absolutely brilliant psychometrician in the Department of Educational Psychology at Texas A&M University—to create an instrument that would measure not only someone's emotional intelligence, but also their personality type and innate vulnerability to stress. That instrument—the Educator Assessment of Social and Emotional Learning (EASEL)—has become the data-based backbone of our EQ-uipped Classroom SEL curriculum. As we've analyzed the data collected in norming the EASEL, we've been amazed at the correlations that emerge between personality types, stress management styles, and innate capacities for self-awareness and empathy. Since what we can measure, we can grow, the EQ-uipped Classroom curriculum seeks to build the SEL toolbox, both within the teacher and in his or her sphere of influence.

Our clinical team also partnered with Dr. Gwen Webb-Hasan, associate professor in the departments of Educational Administration and Human Resource Development at Texas A&M, to ensure that our curriculum bore the quality of social and cultural sensitivity. We have been delighted to have the material incorporated into her graduate courses as she equips the next generation of educational leaders, particularly by challenging them to become more aware of their biases in diverse populations. Diverse populations, in the context of SEL, refer not only to the standard demographic variables, but also to personality types and coping styles.

My continued research into SEL ties together almost everything I learned in my training as a therapist. Being an effective therapist is the ultimate exercise in SEL, as each therapy session consists of a fifty-minute continuum of questions: "What am I thinking and feeling in this moment? How do I regulate it in this moment? What is the client thinking and feeling in this moment? How do I intervene in this moment? And this moment . . . and this moment . . . and this moment?" Now I see why I was so exhausted after each session, especially in those early years, when I wasn't accustomed to this level of mental and emotional analysis.

Finally, my SEL research bears relevance to me not just as a school psychologist with a background in mental assessment, not just as a practicing psychotherapist, but also as an individual who has endured life-long struggles with depression, anxiety, and the damaging effects of trauma. My personal practice of SEL interventions has taught me that the difficult yet courageous work of continually digging deeper to reveal the authentic self while reducing the hidden/unknown self is not without life-changing benefits to the practitioner. This is the proverbial peeling of the layers of the onion to reveal that at the onion's core is yet another onion. I thought I had worked through most of my junk in the therapy sessions of my early twenties. Then I got married, and that relational connection peeled another layer. Right when I thought most of my junk was gone, we had our first child, and that relational connection peeled another layer. Then we had our second child. Then our third. And then we adopted. Then the kids started graduating high school and leaving home. Meanwhile, I started working in schools with students who had significant behavioral and emotional challenges. With each new major adjustment came a new layer of awareness: "Oh, wait. Here's a level of anger/sadness/anxiety you haven't experienced in a long time. Wonder what that's about?" As we say in therapy, there is almost always more grist for the mill when you're paying attention to life.

My Crossroad: Does SEL Really Exist?

My attraction to University of Toronto professor Dr. Jordan Peterson began on a cool Saturday evening in October 2016. Texas climate doesn't offer us too many cool evenings in October, so in something of a *carpe diem* move, I opted to study on our back patio with a kettle of hot water and a tea strainer filled with green tea. I had just started my hot-tea phase, having been converted from high-octane coffee to the less caffeinated substitute by my wife's evangelism. "Caffeine artificially stimulates your adrenal system. It's not good for you," she would tell me with overtones of concern likely arising from the Styrofoam coffee cup that had been glued to my right hand since I was in my early twenties. "You should try hot teas. They are so much gentler to your system."

I was in the early stages of developing the EASEL at that point, and I knew that I wanted to include a personality measure as part of the instrument, but I hadn't yet decided on the specifics. As I opened my laptop that evening, I was intrigued by an email from one of my colleagues.

Date: October 22, 2016
Subject line: Jordan Peterson

Hey Adam,
You need to check out this video. I think you'll appreciate his discussions of the Big 5.
https://www.youtube.com/watch?v=MBWyBdUYPgk.

You're welcome,
Mike

The Big 5 refers to a theory—presently, *the* theory—based on the statistical analysis of personality data. This theory uses common language to describe five dimensions of personality: openness to experience, conscientiousness, extraversion, agreeableness, and neuroticism. The Big 5 Theory makes connections between these domains and the traits that routinely accompany them; for example, extraversion usually includes a level of assertiveness. The EASEL personality domain is based on the Big 5 Model. I opened the link to Jordan Peterson's YouTube channel and found the video entitled "Personality Lecture 20: Biology & Traits: Orderliness/Disgust/Conscientiousness."

Four minutes into the video I was utterly blown away by Dr. Peterson's depth and breadth of knowledge of personality constructs and how we measure them. Captivated, I binge-watched more of his lectures, some on mythology, others on the collective unconscious, and a few on man's search for meaning. I drank lots of green tea that evening, and in the weeks and videos that followed, I branched into white and orange teas. Turmeric and ginger teas, I learned, decrease inflammation. A small study showed that drinking three cups per day of hibiscus tea lowered blood pressure. Coffee with two sugars never offered such hope.

My initial attraction matured to full-blown man crush in May 2017. It happened with Jordan's (we were on a first-name basis by then) "Biblical Series 1: Introduction to the Idea of God." That was when I realized that our stars were aligned, and we were, in fact, a match made in heaven: me, a psychologist and lay clergy, and him, a psychologist with a keen interest in spirituality. It was meant to be.

Never before had I heard anyone exegete a sacred religious text in evolutionary and psychological terms and still argue with such clarity for deep and compelling meaning in the human experience. Jordan spoke from his extensive study of personality theory and the data coded into our collective myth stories to suggest that the garden of Eden is a symbol for order and the comfort of that which is known. The fall from the garden represents the terror of humanity's being thrust into the chaos of the unknown. Subsequently, the human experience derives most meaning, he proposed, in the fine balance between having access to the comfort of order and that which is known *and* the courage to face the chaos and terror of the unknown. By way of example, that which is known would be our primary relational attachments, and the unknown could be broken or new relationships. What I found to be particularly interesting was his conclusion that too much safety leads to stagnation and complacency; too much chaos leads to maladaptive relativism and the over-working of our coping systems, which leads to the eventual decline of mental health.

Mind blown. He had me at "the paradox of a walled garden," but I couldn't get enough. In the meantime, I would devour every word of his Maps of Meaning, which surely he wrote with me in mind. He was the tea leaves to my hot water. Nothing—and I mean nothing—could ever tear us apart.

Except his views on emotional intelligence.

"It's very difficult to find a discipline that's more susceptible to fads than educational psychology," Jordan explained in one of his undergraduate lectures on the measure of intelligence. "Generally speaking, each fad is worse than the previous one."

This was the proverbial needle scratching across the record that told me something was about to go horribly wrong. I never saw it coming.

"The whole point of having a word is that it defines some

things and doesn't define other things," he continued. "When Gardner came up with the idea of multiple intelligences, it was just utter nonsense. Talents are not necessarily intelligence. If [being able to dance well and solving math problems] are both intelligences, people who could dance better would also be better at doing double-digit math problems in their head. For something to be one phenomenon, the things that are sub-sumed under the definition have to be highly correlated. When you control for IQ and certain personality traits, this so-called 'emotional intelligence' drives absolutely zero percent of the variability in predicting outcomes that we know intelligence will predict, like academic achievement. There's no such thing as emotional intelligence—what they're calling emotional intel-ligence is really just the personality trait of agreeableness."

Oh, Jordan. How could he? After all the cups of tea I've shared with him, how could he possibly question the validity of so many years of my work?

And just like that, our six-month, one-way bromance was over. Paradise lost. He could never again be Jordan to me, but would from now on be simply "Peterson." I'd never man-crushed before, and I don't know that I ever will again. I still enjoy the occasional cup of English Breakfast, but it was the coffee at the gas station at the intersection of Rock Prairie and Wellborn, a specialty brew labeled "Jet Fuel," that got me through the breakup.

It may be my artificially stimulated adrenal system talking now, but I am willing to concede that education and fads do seem to go hand in hand. If you've been in the field for more than twenty-three years, consider these terms: alignment, authentic pedagogy, portfolio-based assessment, inquiry-based teaching, school-to-work movement, cooperative learning, black cultural learning styles, and brain-based teaching. Did you roll your eyes at any of these? Might some of these terms represent a fad in education?

Let's take it a step further: If emotional intelligence—and by implication, SEL—doesn't really exist, or is just a fad, then what are we to make of the wealth of other research that touts emotional intelligence as a key factor in academic, behavioral, and vocational success? Is it all just a sham? Is SEL really worth pursuing?

Throughout my training as a psychologist, psychometrician, behavior interventionist, and therapist, I was drilled in the ethic of using only validated measuring tools and interventions to ends that made clinical sense. I didn't have the real-world "oh-so-this-is-what-they-were-warning-me-about" moment until my second year working as a school psychologist, in 2003.

Prior to the 2004 reauthorization of the Individuals with Disabilities Education Act (IDEA), learning disabilities were diagnosed in public school using what was referred to as the "discrepancy model." In a nutshell, a child's IQ was compared to their achievement scores in a handful of core academic areas, and if the IQ was sixteen points higher than their standard score in a measured academic area, the child was said to have met criteria for special services as a student with a learning disability. A few administrators on the campuses I served figured out that students' IQ scores tended to be higher when they were measured with a brief, non-verbal IQ test, signaling that the test's validity and reliability should be in question. The benefit, though, was that a higher IQ score meant we were more likely to find the sixteen-point qualifying discrepancy, meaning that identified students were exempt from state testing. Some saw it as a win-win: The child gets services, and the campus no longer carries the burden of their test score.

All in all, what it boiled down to was using bad tests to mis-identify students as having learning disabilities. It just felt dirty, and as soon as I connected those dots, I no longer did it, despite the pressure from ill-informed administrators. I think it was a familiar case of good-hearted educators, driven by the proverbial pressures from above, succumbing to poor decision-making.

By the time IDEA was reauthorized in 2004, over 50 percent of children receiving special education services in the United States were qualified under the diagnosis of "Learning Disabled," a reality that provided statistical evidence that children were being misdiag-nosed and over-identified. Fortunately, IDEA's reauthorization also provided new guidelines for the assessment of learning disabilities, moving from the discrepancy model to a pattern of strengths and weaknesses on a cross-battery assessment (more on that later).

A similar ethic is said to guide best practice in the selection of classroom instruction: Use only those strategies that have been supported by science. "Research-based" is the exact language we cite. In light of the criticisms raised by the likes of Peterson, our research and clinical teams were faced with a sober task: We first had to establish an ethical roadmap that granted us a clear con-science to create the EASEL assessment (to measure SEL), and then design a curriculum to train children and adults to develop this capacity which may not, in fact, exist.

As evidenced by the book that you are now reading, we did find that ethical roadmap, and the route winds us through the his-tory of intelligence testing, emotional intelligence testing, actu-arial validity, and clinical validity. We feel good about it. Really good, in fact. We believe SEL is both valid (if not actuarially, then certainly clinically) and necessary for the well-being of both adults and students.

Moving Forward

Before I preview the chapters ahead, my gut tells me this is a good time to render a concession. Forgive my bluntness, but I suspect not everyone is between these covers by choice. Some of you had an overachieving department chair or counselor who cornered your principal, pushing the question "Wouldn't it be a great idea if our whole campus did a book study on SEL?" And there went your Thursday afternoons. Even if you didn't have a truckload of papers to grade and sixty-eight emails to send, spending your time reading a book like this probably would fall way down on your to-do list. Like *way* down there, somewhere between "scrub the baseboards" and "journal about your worst breakup."

Well, I have good news for you, my friend—I feel your pain and offer you a salve: You can just get down and dirty. At the end of each chapter, you'll find a page titled "The Down and Dirty," which will contain five to seven bullet points summarizing each chapter (CliffsNotes, anyone?).

In Chapter 1, we'll start by examining two case studies that illustrate the importance of SEL. Then we'll explore how SEL even became a thing, starting with Binet's first IQ test in the early 1900s, then moving to Howard Gardner's theory of multiple intelligences in the 1980s. We'll look at Daniel Goleman's 1995 book *Emotional Intelligence* and the establishment of the Collaborative for Academic, Social, and Emotional Learning (CASEL). This history is important, particularly in response to the social scientists who argue that emotional intelligence doesn't even exist.

Chapter 2 begins an analysis of four of the five core elements of SEL. What and where are emotions, exactly, and what role do they serve in the human experience? What do I know about my personality type? (Spoiler alert: Our innate personality structure factors *significantly* in how we relate to ourselves and with others. For example, people who score high on the Neuroticism scale are more likely to feel but less likely to regulate their emotions well.) What role does our individual experience of stress play in how we understand—or don't understand—ourselves?

Chapter 3 moves into an exploration of self-regulatory skills. Once I've identified my emotional palate, my personality type, and my innate vulnerability to stress, how do I know when I need to intervene with myself? What does self-intervention look like?

Once I have a basic understanding of how to recognize and manage my own emotions, I am now more capable of understanding emotions in others. How do I know others? Is it possible to know the personality of a group? Empathy is grown via the attention we pay to the language we receive from others: verbal, paraverbal, and non-verbal. Chapter 4 explores empathy.

Having increased my capacity to see, listen, and feel with the eyes, ears, and heart of another, how do I then engage the other(s) most productively? Chapter 5 is about social skills. When we think "social skills," most of us think basics, like smiling and maintaining eye contact when shaking someone's hand. However, the application of advanced social skills is much more nuanced. Empathy is developed in attention to the language we receive, but social skills are developed in the language we express. Communication styles are a central concept. We'll also discuss conflict resolution, which is an often overlooked but must-have social skill. (If you score high on the Agreeableness personality scale of the EASEL, conflict resolution may be particularly difficult for you.)

Formally implementing SEL on a classroom, campus, or district level is a very doable undertaking. Chapter 6 covers the basics, from the theoretical questions that need to be answered initially to the pragmatics of getting up and running. The point of all this is to answer these questions: What is social and emotional intelligence? Why does it matter?

Are you ready to jump in? Honestly, I don't blame you if you are not; increasing one's emotional intelligence is not for cowards. But you are bold and courageous, so let's get started.

CHAPTER 1

Why Social and Emotional Learning?

Success in school admits of things other than intelligence;
to succeed in his studies, one must have qualities which
depend on attention, will, and character.

—Alfred Binet, creator of the first IQ test

Emotional intelligence could save your life. Literally. Consider the case of former United States Army General James Lee Dozier, who graduated from West Point Academy in 1956. Following his tour of duty in Vietnam, General Dozier was serving as the Chief of Staff at a NATO land force headquarters in Verona, Italy, in 1981.

At approximately 6 p.m. on December 17, four men posing as plumbers entered his apartment in Verona and overpowered him. He initially resisted, but then opted for compliance the moment he saw his wife being held at gunpoint. His captors left his wife handcuffed to a table in the apartment, but they covered his head with a pillowcase, stuffed him into a cardboard refrigerator box, and proceeded to disorient him while in transport to the designated holding-place, an apartment ninety kilometers away in Padua.

What followed were forty-two days of torture—a controlled, sustained explosion of traumatic stress. General Dozier was confined to a windowless room, where he was chained to a steel cot that was under the constant glare of an electric light bulb. He was forced to listen to a continuous stream of loud music through headphones that were taped to his head. He experienced temporal loss of time, grossly disrupted circadian sleep rhythms, and permanent hearing damage.

His captors, he would soon learn, were members of the Red Brigades, a left-wing terrorist organization who had grown angry at the good diplomatic relations between the United States and Italy. They targeted General Dozier because of his high-profile military standing in the country and his association with NATO. While the Red Brigades issued international communications acknowledging that General Dozier was in their captivity, they never established terms for his release. Instead, their communication consisted of the disgruntled rants of a terrorist organization expressing its dissatisfaction with the political state of world affairs. Given the absence of terms for General Dozier's release, most involved presumed that the Red Brigades had no intention of releasing him; they were simply holding him hostage to gain international attention and would kill him when that attention waned.

Let's analyze the details of General Dozier's case through the lens of emotional intelligence (or, social and emotional learning—SEL—as we like to refer to it in schools), as his case offers a textbook illustration of the value of well-implemented SEL. First, the instant General Dozier saw his wife's life at risk, he knew he would have to manage his thoughts and feelings for both of their safety. That behavioral protocol—identifying and managing his intense emotions—continued through his captivity. **These are components one and two of SEL: self-awareness and self-regulation.**

Having shown the capacity to identify and regulate his emotions, General Dozier knew that he would first have to understand his captors if there was any chance he could influence them. He listened to their nuanced use of language, their references to the media, and he looked for patterns in their behavior as they interacted with him and each other. One guard seemed more inclined to discuss soccer. Two leaders always ate with their guns on the table. Their collective mood elevated when they saw that they were referenced in national media, and they became irritable when they were not mentioned for time periods greater than four days. **This is component three of SEL: social awareness, or empathy**.

Finally, General Dozier kept an extremely consistent daily routine within the confines of his captivity to ease his captors' anxiety; his schedule made him very predictable (and, therefore, safer) to his captors. He always made a point to speak calmly and respectfully, without antagonizing his captors in any way. He talked about non-political topics, and he regularly expressed concern about his wife, whom they had left bound and chained in their apartment. He knew he was making progress building a relational connection when they honored his request to lower the music's volume in his headphones and agreed to play classical rather than rock music. **This is component four of SEL: relationship skills.**

In the end, because he was self-aware and self-regulated his emotions, and because he was socially aware and used effective relational skills, General Dozier was able to act adaptively when his rescuers arrived. Even though a gun was pointed to his head when Italian police entered the apartment, not a single shot was fired by anyone. General Dozier knew to remain calm and to stay low during the ninety seconds of chaos in which his captors were overwhelmed by the rescue force. **This is component five of SEL: responsible decision-making**.

"It's just like combat," he would later say. "You do the best you can in the moment rather than worrying about what might happen."

Ultimately, it was not General Dozier's command of the many troops under his leadership that saved his life, but his command of himself. Dozier would go on to complete a successful military career, being awarded the Army Distinguished Service Medal, the Silver Star, and the Purple Heart, among other highly prestigious decorations.

Maybe the case of General Dozier seems too far removed from your day-to-day role as an educator for your buy-in. You might be wondering, *"Great. But what does this discussion have to do with the lesson plans I haven't yet prepared for tomorrow and the ever-increasing scope of what's being asked of me as an educator?"* Fair enough. I would invite you, then, to consider this second and final case involving the educator Jason Seaman. While the details of Jason Seaman's case are different than General Dozier's (the sustained length of the trauma, in particular), both cases illustrate the relationship between stress and emotional intelligence.

Mr. Seaman, a twenty-nine-year-old science teacher at Indiana's West Noblesville Middle School and former defensive lineman for Southern Illinois University, entered his classroom on May 25, 2018, starting his day off like any other. His students would take what would be their final science test of the school year.

I can't say for sure, but I'm willing to bet that Mr. Seaman had engaged his students or colleagues in discussion about the shooting in Santa Fe, Texas, that left thirteen dead and ten injured just a week before. I know that 130 miles to the northeast of Santa Fe, we in Bryan/College Station, Texas, were still processing the event and at various stages of grieving.

As Mr. Seaman's students took their test that morning, one student asked to be excused from class. He probably just requested a restroom break, but the details aren't clear. What we do know is that moments later, that student returned to the classroom armed with .22 and .45 caliber handguns and immediately opened fire.

"Mr. Seaman started running at him," a student witness reported. "He tackled him to the ground. We were all hiding in the back of the classroom behind some desks, and then Mr. Seaman was yelling to call 911, to get out of the building as fast as we could, so we ran out."

Mr. Seaman's actions were immediate and decisive, but the damage was done. Before Mr. Seaman could even reach the shooter, seven rounds struck a female student in the face, neck, hands, and chest. As he rushed the student, Mr. Seaman was shot three times, once in the abdomen, once in the hip, and once in the forearm. He was able to disarm and detain the student until the school resource officer arrived to assist only moments after the initial shots were fired. Mr. Seaman was taken by ambulance to the Indiana University Hospital, where he made a full recovery. The wounded female student was also hospitalized in critical condition, yet she was expected to recover after having sustained collapsed lungs, a broken jaw, and significant nerve damage.

As we did with General Dozier's case, let's study the details of Mr. Seaman's case in the context of SEL. It's important for us to remember, though, that while General Dozier had forty-two days to fine-tune his SEL skill set as his traumatic stress evolved, Mr. Seaman's experience was an acute, immediate blast of terror in which he had just a handful of seconds to act. With Mr. Seaman's case, we'll start at the end of the trauma and work our way back toward the beginning to find the SEL lesson.

We know that Mr. Seaman demonstrated responsible deci-sion-making (SEL component five), as evidenced by the fact that he subdued and contained the shooter. Protecting children's lives and maintaining safety always represents sound and responsible decision-making. But given the moment's urgency, it's highly unlikely that Mr. Seaman's navigation through the first four SEL components was a conscious process: "Because I feel angry and afraid that a student is shooting (self-awareness), I'll control that emotion with two deep, strong breaths (self-regulation); mean-while, it is likely that the shooter feels anger, given the weapons in his hands (social awareness/empathy), and since I don't have the liberty of talking to him about his anger, I will intervene physi-cally (responsible decision-making)."

Nope, not likely. Rather, the heart of our SEL lesson from Mr. Seaman is found in his words during a subsequent television interview: "I care deeply about my students and their well-being," he noted to the reporter. "That's why I did what I did that day."

My goodness. That is powerful.

What we learn from Mr. Seaman is that when we don't have the luxury of time to consciously engage our SEL skills, our

core-level beliefs—our deepest values, fears, biases, and preju-
dices—drive our behavior automatically. Fortunately for the students in Mr. Seaman's classroom that day, his core-level belief was
that his students mattered above all, and it was that foundational
belief that resulted in his automatic action to risk his life to save
his students' lives.

So, there you have it, without hyperbole: The case of General Dozier illustrates that well-developed SEL could save your
life, and the case of Mr. Seaman illustrates that our actions are
driven by deeply embedded value systems and/or biases. SEL is
relevant whether you are a United States General on an overseas
deployment or a seventh-grade middle school teacher adminis-
tering a final exam.

The Broad Application of SEL: Life Givers Versus Life Suckers

While General Dozier and Mr. Seaman displayed a life-saving
understanding and implementation of SEL, you might be wondering what role SEL plays in your professional, as well as your
personal life. Let us not embrace the false assumption that SEL is
only about being prepared for crises such as those just presented.
Far from it. We'll explore the relationship between aggression,
violence, and SEL in Chapter 7, but this book is not centrally
about preparing ourselves to deal with active school shooters.

That kind of preparation, sadly, is more urgent now than it
has ever been, but SEL has *so* much more to offer us. SEL is
essential to our capacity to live adaptively in our daily lives—days
that don't involve hostage situations or active shooters. The classroom teacher dealing with postpartum depression as she returns

to work from maternity leave? Exercise in SEL. The angry parent who uses social media to air his misinformed conclusions of you? Exercise in SEL. Your passive-aggressive neighbor who still leaves his garbage cans on your driveway even after you've politely asked twice that he not do so? Exercise in SEL. Your spouse, who twenty-three years later still doesn't know the correct direction to mount the toilet paper roll? Exercise in SEL.

The list could go on, even down to each moment-to-moment interaction we have with any other human being who, in whatever way and for whatever reason, evokes within us a potentially conflict-producing emotion. In every case, the successful return to mental well-being is dependent on our ability to know and regulate ourselves, and to understand and interact with others.

> "The successful return to mental well-being is dependent on our ability to know and regulate ourselves, and to understand and interact with others."

I was in my early thirties when I finished my doctoral degree and started working as a school psychologist. It was the early 2000s, and I was jumping into the world of education eager to make a difference but also feeling overwhelmed by my lack of experience in school systems. Stress, I was learning, is not only a feeling our bodies produce when we wonder whether we can deal effectively with a new situation, but also an energy that mobilizes us to respond. To cope with my stress, I searched for mentorship from professionals in the district who had a long history of service in the schools. I hoped they could speak from their years of experience to give me guidance, shortcuts, or anything else that offered me hope that I might grow older well and live to tell about it. I never would have predicted what that search revealed: two groups of near-retirees, distributed neatly into two categories. Group One: Life Givers, and Group Two: Life Suckers.

Fortunately, the Life Givers were by far the bigger group. They were approaching their retirement with mixed degrees of sadness and excitement, but also with a deep sense of having run the race well. Some had plans for significant life changes, and others said they would like to stick around in any capacity possible since they couldn't imagine a life apart from students. As seasoned veterans, they were filled with joy about the immeasurable investment they had made in countless individuals, young and not-so-young, over the course of their careers. They often reminisced, with a smile and distant look in their eye, as they shared with me (ever so generously) the lessons they had learned along the way.

In contrast, the Life Suckers were the much smaller group. Unlike the Life Givers, the Life Suckers were bitter and cynical, and they seemed to be approaching their retirement as a get-out-of-jail-free card that was not actually free and came *way* too late in the game. They seemed to go out of their way to make sure that nothing they said was ever contaminated by an encouraging word or any sense of hope or optimism. They routinely made subtle and not-so-subtle comments that degraded and demeaned children and adults. They were miserable.

I was baffled: How could anyone end up at this stage in their career, so deeply soaked in bitterness and resentment? What went wrong for them, and at what point? How did they not have the wherewithal to take note and act at the first indication that their hope was circling the drain?

Looking back, I'm convinced that the variable that predicted the differences between the two groups was not the narrative of their

> "I was baffled: How could anyone end up at this stage in their career, so deeply soaked in bitterness and resentment? What went wrong for them, and at what point?"

professional experience. It wasn't like the Life Givers had somehow lucked into having been dealt thirty years of more playable cards—ideal students from ideal families being educated on ideal campuses by ideal faculty, year after year. I knew for a fact that many of the Life Givers had invested long windows of their careers in high-needs educational settings. I also don't think it was correlated to their education or professional training: Both groups had individuals with graduate degrees from prestigious universities. It wasn't a factor of sheer intelligence, either; the Life Givers weren't all in the genius range, and the Life Suckers weren't all dull. Indeed, high IQs were present in both groups.

Observations of Mentor Candidates

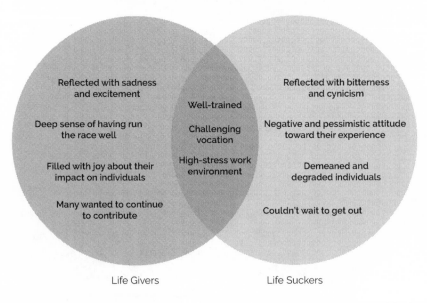

Figure 1: Life Givers Versus Life Suckers

If it wasn't any of that, then, what *was* it that explained the variance? After fifteen years of research and clinical practice, I'm convinced that the deciding factor that sorted the Life Givers from the Life Suckers was emotional intelligence. Life Givers have heart smarts. They intuitively understand the necessity of emotional hygiene, and they practice it just as routinely as they bathe their bodies and brush their teeth. At some point along the way, Life Givers somehow figure out that their emotions are packets of energy and information, and how they process and regulate their emotion positively correlates with their quality of life. They also learn that since their emotional life is *that* important, then everyone else's must be also, and how they interact with others is pertinent to ensuring the best possible outcomes.

I knew three things at that early point in my career: I really enjoyed my work in schools, I wanted to be in it for the long run, and I wanted to land where the Life Givers had landed. I would learn very quickly that the soon-to-retire Life Givers were not just the kind of professionals I wanted to become, they were the kind of people I wanted to be.

What I observed almost twenty years ago was the actual playing-out of the vast body of emotional intelligence research that consistently tells us that individuals who live emotionally intelligent lives experience a variety of benefits: greater job satisfaction, higher sustainability, increased productivity, physical and psychological longevity, and the capacity to thrive in high-stress and high-demand jobs. There are benefits apart from work, too. People who live emotionally intelligent lives report a greater sense of overall well-being, a deeper sense

> "individuals who live emotionally intelligent lives experience a variety of benefits"

of satisfaction with life, and a deeper sense of peace with their journey. So, no, SEL is not just about being prepared for crises; it's about deliberately living well.

> "A greater sense of overall well-being, a deeper sense of satisfaction with life, and a deeper sense of peace with their journey. So, no, SEL is not just about being prepared for crises; it's about deliberately living well."

We know that SEL benefits adults cross-situationally, but can the same be said of kids? Joseph Durlak's 2011 meta-analysis rendered results that are not particularly surprising. He and his Chicago-based research team reviewed 213 universal SEL programs involving 270,034 kindergarten through high school students. Compared to controls, students who had received SEL education demonstrated significantly improved social and emotional skills, attitudes, behavior, and (here's the kicker) academic performance, reflected by an eleven-percentile-point gain in achievement. In sum, then, we can confidently say that when students can accurately identify and regulate their feelings, and when they demonstrate social awareness and social skills, then they engage in responsible decision-making. Therefore, the students demonstrate both social and academic growth.

> "I have become a firm believer that the best academic or behavioral intervention for every student is an adult living a life characterized by physical well-being and emotional intelligence."

So, yes, SEL is widely encompassing and relevant to so much more than just gun violence. In fact, I would summarize my work in schools over the past twenty years by saying that I have become a firm believer that the best academic or behavioral intervention for every student is an adult living a life characterized by physical well-being and emotional intelligence. Unlike IQ, which is a relatively stable trait (aspects of which peak in our early twenties and decline as we age), SEL is a skill set that we can continually grow and retain. This is good news: Our prognosis to be Life Givers is excellent.

Measuring Intelligence

If you lived in Philadelphia, say in 1843, and you wanted to know your child's cognitive ability, you would have made an appointment with Dr. Samuel Morton, physician and professor of anatomy at Pennsylvania Medical College, who had all that was needed to answer your question: the right hands, a tape measure, and a caliper.

"Good morning," Dr. Morton would greet you in his office. "What brings you in today?"

"Well, Dr. Morton," you would answer, "I heard a public lecture last night by a politician named Horace Mann. He spoke at great length about the changes he would like to see in schools. He talked about all kids being in the classroom together so they could have a common experience, and to give opportunity to the less fortunate. His words excited me, and I thought about my daughter. I'm here to see if you think she's smart enough to do well in school. Can you measure her intelligence?"

"Very well, then," Dr. Morton would say. He would turn toward your daughter and motion her toward a table. "Sit right up here, young lady."

After your daughter hopped on his table, Dr. Morton would begin the intelligence exam by moving his hands across all aspects of your daughter's scalp, looking for irregularities in her skull structure. He would jot down a few notes and then reach for his tape measure. A measure of cranial circumference. A measure of pupillary distance. If your daughter's case warranted, Dr. Morton would use calipers to measure distances between locations on her skull.

"Ah, yes," Dr. Morton, would say in a summarizing tone as he reviewed his numbers to offer you a diagnosis. "Bumps toward the temporal lobe suggest a predisposition toward alimentiveness and philoprogentiveness."

So, now you know that your daughter loves food and will probably love her offspring. Great. But no help with regard to your initial question.

"Yes, doctor," you say with some degree of impatience. "But what about her intelligence?"

"Oh, her intelligence? Well, I would say it's probably about average."

"And how do you know, doctor, that her intelligence is about average?"

"By the circumference of her head. It's about average, so we might deduce that her intelligence is also about average."

"So, do you think she will fare well in school? Does she have the ability?"

"Maybe. Then again, maybe not. Hard to tell." And that would be that from your visit with Dr. Morton.

Not only was Dr. Morton a physician and professor, he was also a practitioner of phrenology, which was the (very soft) science of rendering personality diagnostics based on the bumps on a person's skull. Phrenologists believed that an individual's mental capacities could be determined by measuring the area of the skull that overlies the area of the brain that was thought to house the given capacity. All in all, it was a straightforward process that rendered grossly invalid results. At that time, though, it was about the only show in town.

The roots of formal, statistically sound psychometric assessment had soil in which to sprout thanks to Alfred Binet's failed research in subconscious automatism (hypnotism) and the French government's desire to educate all children. Binet's first formal research position was at Jean-Martin Charcot's neurological laboratory in Paris. Charcot's early research in subconscious automatism promised tremendous benefits for its practitioners, and Binet published several articles citing the value of Charcot's work. Upon independent external peer review, however, Charcot's studies were found to be flawed by poor methodology, forcing Binet to publicly recant his findings. A dejected Binet turned to the study of child development for solace, a field he found particularly relevant given the recent births of his two daughters, Madeleine and Alice. Over the course of the next twenty years, Binet would come to be recognized as an expert in the field, prolifically publishing in the areas of human development and social psychology.

Meanwhile, the French government passed a law mandating school attendance for children ages six to fourteen, and they soon faced the challenge of effectively educating children of diverse cognitive abilities. They approached Binet: What test should we give to identify children thought to have learning differences so that we might offer them appropriate instruction?

Binet's years of working with children taught him that at certain ages, most children can answer certain questions correctly. He partnered with Theodore Simon, a medical student, to create a series of questions that an examiner could expect most children to answer correctly at specific ages. Could a child track a beam of light when it shone across a wall? Point to various body parts when asked? Repeat a long series of digits? Construct a sentence from three given words—dog, city, and treasure? More challenging items asked children to repeat a number series in reverse order or to answer questions based on ambiguous stimuli: "My neighbor has been receiving strange visitors. He has received in turn a doctor, a lawyer, and then a priest. What might be taking place?"

The child's performance on the test could be compared to a mental age, which is the age at which the average child would be expected to know the answers. The mathematic relationship between a child's mental and chronological age was central to computing the child's intelligence quotient: Divide mental age by physical age, multiply times one hundred, and voilà, you have IQ. For example, if a child scored at a mental age of twelve while being chronologically ten years old, the child's IQ would be 120 (12/10 x 100 = 120). The resulting test and scoring system that arose from that initial endeavor commissioned by the French government would become the Binet-Simon Measuring Scale for Intelligence, the first formal measure of IQ.

Across the Atlantic, American psychologist Henry Goddard had been appointed Director of Research at the Vineland Training School for Feeble-Minded Girls and Boys. Goddard translated the Binet-Simon Measuring Scale for Intelligence into English and found it helpful in identifying children with intellectual disabilities. In 1910, he advocated for a system of classifying levels of intellectual disability: Those with an IQ of 51–70 would be referred to as morons, 26–50 would be referred to as imbeciles, and 0–25 would be idiots. It sounds shocking to hear, I know, but in Goddard's day, those terms had none of the negative connotations they do today. The eventual stigma those terms came to communicate led to their being replaced by the terms "mild, moderate, and severe mental retardation." Then, the eventual stigma *those* terms came to communicate led to their being replaced by the present nomenclature of "mild, moderate, and severe intellectual disability."

By 1916, Stanford Education professor Lewis Terman normed the translated Binet-Simon scales with an American population, thereby allowing American examiners to make a truer apples-to-apples comparison when establishing standard and percentile scores among examinees. The newly normed instrument became known as the Stanford-Binet Intelligence Test, and is still widely used and in its fifth edition at the time of this writing.

Fairly early on, psychometricians began to wonder what, exactly, was going on in the brain that was being measured. Surely, repeating a number series measured a different cognitive skill than, say, stacking colored blocks to recreate patterned designs. English psychologist Charles Spearman was the first to apply formal statistical analysis to explore correlations between tests and among test items. When he analyzed the statistical relationships among school grades across seemingly unrelated subjects in individual children, he found strong positive correlates; children who scored higher in math also scored higher in language arts and history. There must be some common cognitive factor, he reasoned, that would explain the correlation—some innate general intellectual ability that fueled all mental tasks. He named that general ability "g" for "general factor," and he proposed that when we're talking about intelligence, we're talking about *g*. "One can talk of mind power," he noted, "in much the same manner as about horse power."

Intelligence is intellectual power, or intellectual work divided by time. The child who, in ten years, demonstrates the intellectual abilities that the average child needs twelve years to demonstrate is clearly advanced on the time track; in contrast, the child who needs eighteen years to demonstrate the intellectual abilities that the average child needs only five years to develop is clearly delayed. One of Spearman's students, David Wechsler, would go on to develop what have become two of the most commonly used IQ measures, the Wechsler Intelligence Scale for Children (now in its fifth edition), and the Wechsler Adult Intelligence Scale (now in its fourth edition).

So, Binet, then Goddard, then Terman, then Spearman and Wechsler. The final stop worth making in the developmental journey of psychoeducational assessment is based on the work of three American psychologists, Raymond B. Cattell, John L. Horn, and John B. Carroll. Their work is central to the current process used in the evaluation of learning disabilities. All three suspected that while a general factor of intelligence may drive some aspect of broad cognitive ability, surely, we can find more specific subskills that factor in to the variety of intellectual tasks we face on a day-to-day basis. Their resulting body of work is referred to as the Cattell-Horn-Carroll (CHC) theory. Cattell endorsed two forms of ability that emerge as a function of age: fluid and crystallized. Fluid intelligence involves the capacity for reason (like figuring out the best route to drop off your child before picking up the dry cleaning on the other side of town) and the ability to learn new things, and it tends to decline in late adulthood. Crystallized intelligence involves knowledge that has come from past experiences (like understanding what you are reading on this page), and it tends to increase or remain stable with age.

If you lived in College Station, Texas, say in 2019, and you wanted to know your child's cognitive ability, you would make sure to sit next to me in the bleachers next Friday night, since our boys play football together.

"Hey, Adam," you would start, maybe with some degree of timidity, as the defensive line started pre-game warm-up drills. "I hope you don't mind, but can I ask you a question about testing for learning disabilities? It's about Mark."

"Of course," I would respond.

"Well," you would continue, "he's been struggling academically, and we've tried everything—tutoring, support with homework, we've offered him the moon and the stars as carrots, we've taken away the moon and the stars as sticks. You name it, we've done it. I'm really starting to think that if he could do the work, he would, and I'm wondering if maybe he actually just can't. Maybe he has a learning disability. Do you test for that?"

"Yes, I do test for learning disabilities," I would answer, "and I'd be happy to evaluate him. There are some important things to keep in mind. First, since insurance companies don't deem educational testing medically necessary, they won't pay for it, and it would be an out-of-pocket expense for you. Second, even if I did test and determine that your son has a learning disability, the school district doesn't necessarily have to take my word for it. They might, but they also have the right to conduct their own testing, and it won't cost you anything. And hopefully, before they did that, they would offer him a series of academic interventions first to see how he responds. There is usually a longer wait in the school system, but they do have timelines that keep them accountable. It's a lot to think about, but again, I'd be happy to help. Just let me know."

If you opted to make an appointment in my office, the good news would be that my hands would not need to touch your son's scalp, and I wouldn't use a tape measure or caliper. We know now that the cognitive abilities at the heart of CHC theory predict all kinds of tasks involved in academic endeavor. Processing speed correlates with academic fluency skills; auditory processing correlates with listening comprehension (and the subsequent ability to follow verbal directions); fluid reasoning correlates with applied math problems. Identifying patterns of cognitive and academic strengths and weaknesses (and the potential learning disabilities associated with them) has never before been a more reliable or valid process.

I'll conclude this section on IQ testing by acknowledging that the field of intelligence testing, as data-driven as it is, has been controversial almost from the get-go. Terman and Princeton University psychologist Carl Brigham argued that the collective IQ of the United States was dropping due to the influx of immigrants, and they recommended (among many other unthinkable interventions) that children be segregated by racial identification to decrease the phenomenon of breeding across races. Consider this from Terman:

> High-grade or border-line deficiency ... is very, very common among Spanish-Indian and Mexican families of the Southwest and also among Negroes. Their dullness seems to be racial, or at least inherent in the family stocks from which they come ... Children of this group should be segregated into separate classes ... They cannot master abstractions but they can often be made into

efficient workers ... from a eugenic point of view they constitute a grave problem because of their unusually prolific breeding.

I could go on here, but I'm sure you get the point. IQ testing has been used to harmful ends, and those abuses have created a public relations struggle for the field. We must make no mistake about it, though: Today, intelligence tests are more valid and reliable than any other kind of psychological measurement. IQ as a construct is more valid than any other phenomena we measure in the social sciences. Intellectual abilities are real, they vary across individuals, and they do have predictive qualities.

> "Today, intelligence tests are more valid and reliable than any other kind of psychological measurement."

What about *emotional* intelligence, though? Can the same be said of it, or was Peterson right? Let's move to the second stop in our ethics journey.

Measuring Emotional Intelligence

While Goddard and Terman's work popularized the use of IQ tests in educational and military settings, a psychologist at Teachers College of Columbia University wondered about the utility of such testing in the workforce. As America settled into the throes of its second industrial revolution, labor leaders, business managers, and executives were tasked with the challenge of creating effective work teams from an increasingly diverse population. Edward Thorndike, a psychologist who worked on solving industrial problems, suggested that successful employees would have the ability to understand and manage ideas (abstract intelligence), concrete objects (mechanical intelligence), and people (social intelligence). Could a test be developed, Thorndike wondered, that would increase our "ability to understand and manage men and women and boys and girls, to act wisely in human relations"?

Thelma Hunt answered. As a psychologist at George Washington University, she created one of the earliest measures of social intelligence—the George Washington University Social Intelligence Test. The field immediately recognized that unlike IQ measures, which were fixed models measuring relatively stable traits, measures of social intelligence were more fluid approaches capturing nuanced and dynamic human traits. For example, the most recent version of Dr. Hunt's test includes items that ask respondents to recognize the mental state of a speaker, demonstrate judgment in social situations, and demonstrate a sense of humor. This line of psychoeducational assessment would lay the foundation for current assessments and procedures used to diagnose Autism Spectrum Disorder.

Early on, many in the field of psychology embraced the value of the study of social intelligence. They recognized only by intuition at that point, given the absence of accumulated data, that our internal emotional landscape *must* factor into the ultimate quality of our experience. Even David Wechsler (of the IQ testing hall of fame noted above) suggested that affective—and not just intellectual—aspects of our experience may not just be related, but in fact essential to human achievement. (Wechsler is reported to have recanted this claim later in his career, a detail that speaks to the division that remains in the field about whether emotional intelligence is a viable, measurable construct.)

Fast-forward to 1983 and Howard Gardner's release *of Frames of Mind: The Theory of Multiple Intelligences.* He had touched on the idea of multiple intelligences in his 1973 *The Shattered Mind,* in which he explored the impact of brain trauma on subsequent cognition. *Frames of Mind,* though, represented the formal introduction of his theory of multiple intelligences to the world. Surely, he thought, humans possess a variety of cognitive skills and process information differently from one another, and with skills that are not necessarily correlated. Rather than seeing intelligence as Peterson does, being driven by a single underlying factor (*g*) and subfactors (*Gv, Gs,* etc.), Gardner proposed that we might be better served in understanding intelligence if we consider these modalities: 1) musical-rhythmic; 2) visual-spatial; 3) verbal-linguistic; 4) logical-mathematical; 5) bodily-kinesthetic; 6) interpersonal; 7) intrapersonal; and 8) naturalistic. He concluded that each of these modalities share common underlying factors and meet certain life-function criteria.

The idea was generally well received, but there were detractors. The mixed reaction to Gardner's theory illustrates the importance of distinguishing actuarial versus clinical validity. Before I tell you why reactions to Gardner were mixed, though, let me first explain what I mean when I mention the difference between actuarial and clinical validity in the context of measurement.

A valid test is one that is logically sound and shown to measure what it reports to measure. Actuarial validity is considered the gold standard when establishing a test's validity. Is a given yardstick, for example, truly thirty-six inches? We might say that a yardstick with actuarial validity is one that has, in fact, been measured against many other yardsticks that have proven to be thirty-six inches, and the data shows that our yardstick consistently matches the comparison group.

In contrast, a test's clinical validity is established not so much by proven data, but when we've used the test and found good results. Clinical validity is more of a real-life test, and for the pragmatist, clinical validity is the bottom line. In sum, actuarial validity asks, "*Does the data prove it true?*," while clinical validity asks, "*Does this thing help?*"

Now, back to the mixed reaction to Gardner's theory of multiple intelligences. Opposers of his theory argued that it had no actuarial validity: That is, there was no hard data to verify that these different kinds of intelligences exist, let alone ways to measure them (quite unlike CHC's *g*, *Gs*, etc.). No hard data means no validity. Period. You might think of the opposers, Peterson among them, as embracing the worldview summarized by the quote from American engineer W. Edwards Deming: "In God we trust, all others must bring data."

However, some people—educators, in particular—loved the idea of multiple intelligences. "I don't care what the data does or does not say, they reasoned, now that we know that kids might learn differently, we can diversify our educational strategies to access the strengths of the individual learner and, therefore, increase learning in our classrooms." In other words, the idea of multiple intelligences had "clinical validity," meaning that it was useful in the classroom. More on how clinical validity relates to SEL soon, but first let's finish the timeline of our emotional intelligence journey—by way of Peter Salovey, John Mayer (not the musician), Daniel Goleman, and CASEL.

After Gardner formally brought the idea of multiple intelligences, Peter Salovey and his colleague John Mayer developed a theory of emotional intelligence and authored one of the most widely used measures of emotional intelligence, the

Mayer-Solovey-Caruso Emotional Intelligence Test. Test items require examinees to read emotions in people, landscapes, and designs, and to compare emotions to sensations like lights and colors. They also ask that test-takers determine which emotional strategy would be most effective in a certain social situation.

Although Salovey and Mayer are credited with coining the term "emotional intelligence," it was Daniel Goleman's 1995 New York Times bestselling book *Emotional Intelligence: Why It Can Matter More Than IQ* that solidified the term into the public lexicon. "If your emotional abilities aren't in hand," he wrote, "if you don't have self-awareness, if you are not able to manage your distressing emotions, if you can't have empathy and have effective relationships, then no matter how smart you are, you are not going to get very far."

As Goleman's work was taking the corporate world by storm, we in schools were beginning to see an alarming rate of aggression and violence on our campuses. Could pro-social training be an answer? Thus, SEL entered mainstream education when the Collaborative to Advance Social and Emotional Learning (CASEL) was formed as a national organization to serve as a clearing house, per se, for all things SEL. The organization moved to Chicago in the late 1990s and eventually changed its name to the Collaborative for Academic, Social, and Emotional Learning. A key element of standardization that arose from CASEL was the foundational understanding that SEL would incorporate the following five components:

1. Self-awareness: identifying emotions; accurate self-perception; recognizing strengths; self-confidence; self-efficacy

2. Self-regulation: impulse control; stress management;

self-discipline; self-motivation; goal-setting; organizational skills

3. Social awareness: perspective-taking; empathy; appreciating diversity; respect for others

4. Social/relationship skills: communication; social engagement; relationship building; teamwork; conflict resolution

5. Responsible decision-making: analyzing situations; solving problems; evaluating; reflecting; ethical responsibility

> "Our capacities to recognize and regulate ourselves and others—despite IQ—clearly predict outcomes for individuals and organizations."

So, what started with Edward Thorndike's desire to improve employee performance in an increasingly diverse workplace and Thelma Hunt's attempt to measure emotional intelligence has now become what we refer to as SEL in schools. Though some may still argue against SEL's actuarial validity, its clinical validity cannot be denied: Our capacities to recognize and regulate ourselves and others—despite IQ—clearly predict outcomes for individuals and organizations.

Stick with me. I'll prove it.

Your Very Own IQ and EQ Test

Step into my office, where I will ask you to take a short IQ and EQ test. Bear with me as you think through the answers, and when we're done, you'll see why we went this route. I recommend grabbing a pen and paper to jot down your answers as we go.

The IQ problems are matrices that measure non-verbal reasoning, attention to detail, and visual processing. These are the cognitive skills that predict how well you do things like merge into highway traffic or respond to your daughter's obscure request for a large sum of money. If you don't feel like you did particularly well after you go through them, don't worry about it. Remember, this is only measuring one particular kind of cognitive ability, and this kind might not be your strength. For example, I'm pretty good at crossword puzzles, but I hate sudoku puzzles because I'm terrible at them.

The first item is very straightforward. You have ten seconds to replace the question mark with the best of the responses offered in the second matrix. Don't read on until you have an answer. Remember: ten seconds. Ready, set, go.

IQ Test Item #1

b	b
b	?

a	b	r	m	s

Similarity drives the pattern among the letters presented in IQ Test Item #1. It's a straightforward presentation—nothing really to overthink—and the correct answer is b. I can think of no other interpretations of the matrix that would argue that another response is better. Most people arrive at the correct answer in less than ten seconds, but if it took you the full ten, no problem.

On to IQ Test Item #2. This one is a little more abstract, so you'll have twenty seconds to select your final answer. Again, don't read on until you have chosen your answer. Ready, set, go.

IQ Test Item #2

b	d
p	?

a	R	9	q	m

IQ Test Item #2 draws into relationship the letters b and d, and the letters b and p. One might reason that since the letters b and d are separated by a single letter, the correct answer would be R, because p and r are also separated by a single letter. However, two details argue against R as the correct response. First, the letters b, d, and p in the first matrix are lowercase, and the R presented in the second matrix is uppercase. Second, the letters b, d, and p are presented in the same font, and the letter R is presented in a different font. For IQ Test Item #2, then, the best response is q because the q preserves the pattern of loops facing inward and stems on the outside pointing downward.

You're doing great. Here's the next one, again somewhat more abstract than the previous test item. Again, twenty seconds. Ready, set, go.

IQ Test Item #3

A	Z
E	?

R	B	F	X	V

The best answer to IQ Test Item #3 is V. A and Z represent the outer boundaries of the alphabet, and both E and V are four letters removed from the end. Okay, here's the last one. It's very abstract. Give it thirty seconds, and if you don't know the answer, don't sweat it, just go ahead and read on. Ready, set, go.

IQ Test Item #4

¥		Z	
		?	

2s	SS	{2	&l	HS

I'll explain the correct answer to this one at the end of the chapter. Hang on—later you will understand my rationale for waiting (it has to do with how we respond to some of life's toughest problems).

Now, let's shift to our EQ problems. These will be like the IQ Test Items in that the first one will be straightforward and then they'll get more complex. Read the description below and identify how the person in the story erred, particularly in the context of the five tenets of SEL (self-awareness, self-regulation, social awareness/empathy, social/relationship skills, and responsible decision-making).

You'll have thirty seconds to determine how the subject erred, and for this question, I'd like you to use at least three components of SEL to explain your answer. Ready, set, go.

EQ Test Item #1

A male district-level administrator expresses his frustration with a female campus-level administrator to three other district employees. He asks, "What value does she bring to this district other than her (body parts)?"

Let's consider our answer with the five aspects of SEL in mind. We don't know for sure if the administrator demonstrated self-awareness, but it's not likely. We do know by his inability to express his anger appropriately that he failed at the self-regulation of his emotion. Also, it's unlikely that he had much, if any, social awareness. If he did, he would have been able to consider the perspective of the female employee he was criticizing (and every other female, for that matter) and become aware of how hurtful and grossly inappropriate his words were. Even a modest amount of social skills would have told him that such expressions of anger would destroy any hope of a favorable team dynamic. Finally, he clearly did not engage in responsible decision-making, as evidenced by the fact that he wasn't thinking about his ethical responsibility to the district.

Let's go on to EQ Test Item #2, in which you are asked to identify at least three problems with the email a campus-level administrator sent to her faculty. You have thirty seconds. Ready, set, go.

EQ Test Item #2

Attention faculty:

It has come to my attention that some of you are not turning in lesson plans to your coordinator as we discussed during our last faculty meeting. Remember, WE AGREED THAT THIS WOULD BE THE PROCESS! It frustrates me that SOME OF YOU are making this a problem for everyone. I trust that this WON'T be an issue moving forward.

Dr. Smith

Granted, this administrator does seem to have some self-awareness, as she is able to identify that she's frustrated (that's better than the guy in EQ Test Item #1). It's pretty much downhill from there, though. First, she chose to address the entire faculty for mistakes that only a few made; she would have been much wiser to have simply addressed those few offenders in isolation. This represents a lack of responsible decision-making. Second, SHE CHOSE TO USE CAPS LOCK, WHICH IS ALMOST NEVER A GOOD IDEA, BECAUSE IT COMES ACROSS LIKE SHE IS A SHOUTING, CONDESCENDING JERK WHO LACKS THE LINGUISTIC CAPACITY TO COMMUNICATE EFFECTIVELY USING BIG-GIRL WRITING SKILLS. This represents a lack of self-regulation and social skills. Third, she offers no encouragement, no indication of what the faculty is doing well, and zero positivity. Words of encouragement are often a spoonful of sugar that can help the medicine go down. This represents a lack of empathy, or understanding that her teachers have many demands placed on them, and might have simply forgotten the new requirement. Fourth, the opening and closing are rudely brief. No "Dear Faculty" or "Good morning, everyone." Instead, she goes with "Attention faculty," which makes it sound like she's about to issue a military command. She offers no real closing (even something as simple as "Sincerely" would have warmed things up), and she uses her title with no first name. There is a time for titles in more formal settings (like an Individualized Education Plan meeting, for example), but my experience among colleagues is that "Adam" conveys more friendly and approachable tones than "Dr. Saenz." The opening and closing indicate the lack of empathy and social skills. Those are four things I see. Can you think of anything else?

Okay, now, let's move on to the final EQ test item. This one is much more advanced, so take as long as you'd like to think through it.

EQ Test Item #3

One of your second-grade teachers is returning from maternity leave and although you don't know for sure, you believe she is struggling with postpartum depression. Since you have known her for some years, you know that she is a highly agreeable person. How could her personality style potentially help her in this time, and how might it hinder her? How would personality style potentially help and hinder you in your role of supporting/directing her? Would your preferred stress management style (think fight or flight) complement or compete with hers?

Like I said, this one is more advanced. Most people aren't knowledgeable about their personality types or their stress coping styles (you'll learn a lot more about yours in the next four chapters), so let me jump in here. I'll take it question by question:

- *How would her personality style help and hinder her?*

Since she is highly agreeable (and would score high on the Agreeableness trait on the Big 5 personality theory), she is likely going to be able to connect with others easily. She is probably an ideal team player who is committed to the group dynamic and responds favorably to leadership. However, people who score high on the Agreeableness scale are often prone to be people pleasers who fear disappointing others. She is at risk, then, for not being honest about her needs for fear of being rejected or isolated.

- *How would your personality style help and hinder your role in supporting/directing her?*

Since I score high on the Conscientiousness scale, I would be helpful to her because I could create a list of things to do to help her find out whether she has depression and, if so, how to deal with it. If she couldn't get the list done, I probably would offer to help, since nothing excites us high-Conscientiousness folk more than checking things off our to-do list. However, since I also score low on the Agreeableness scale, I probably wouldn't be relationally engaged enough to approach her with kindness, and I probably would come across as too matter-of-fact, which isn't very helpful when talking about sensitive issues. It's unlikely that I would adequately communicate my concern for her, and since she is high in Agreeableness, she probably would have sensed that right away.

- *Would your preferred stress management style complement or compete with hers?*

My stress management style would probably complement hers. Generally, I am fairly balanced in my capacities to engage and disengage in response to stress. Whether she preferred to respond to stress by engaging or disengaging, I feel confident that I would be able to help her find coping strategies.

It Takes SEL to Teach SEL

Okay, this is where we get real-life. This is where we tie it together: the ethical roadmap involving the history lesson in IQ and EQ, actuarial versus clinical validity, why SEL matters, and how I think SEL is best learned.

Since we know that IQ predicts performance, we can predict that someone who struggled to find the correct answer to IQ Test Item #1 will have an incredibly difficult, if not impossible, time managing the tasks and understanding the relationships associated with leading a classroom. Supervising a campus or district wouldn't even be a consideration. We know both intuitively and empirically that a specified amount of intelligence is necessary to function as a professional educator, and that's part of the reason we ask classroom leaders to have college degrees and campus/district leaders to have graduate degrees. In essence, we have gatekeeping processes that serve the best interest of our students by offering them leadership from adults who have demonstrated the cognitive capacity to keep them safe and to keep them learning. That seems reasonable and straightforward, right?

But here's the thing: We don't hold the same standard for emotional intelligence—there is no equivalent gatekeeper. We might argue that growth plans and eventual terminations serve as gatekeepers to keep adults who lack emotional intelligence out of positions of influence with children, but those are *post hoc* and generally ineffective approaches; most of us know adults who beat the system by hopping from school to school and from district to district. The first two EQ test items I presented above are real cases I've personally encountered in my work in schools. The district-level administrator in EQ Test Item #1, while being placed on paid leave for a long series of ethical violations (including making that comment), secured a job leading another district, and through legal haranguing, received not only a letter of recommendation, but a payout on the balance of his contract.

Let me be clear: I didn't walk you through this chapter simply to tee-up a cynical argument suggesting that schools are filled with emotionally unintelligent adults. My point is that regardless of whether hard data shows that EQ/SEL does, in fact, hold empirical validity, the EQ test items presented here illustrate that having good awareness and regulatory skills is essential for productive outcomes, both for the individual and for the group. When those skills are not in place, students and adults are not safe (at least psychologically, if not also physically), and students don't learn what we hope they will, and probably do learn many things we hope they won't. There is clear clinical validity here.

Since SEL is clearly important, the question then becomes *how* we empower educators and students with the SEL skill set they will need to be successful. There are three main approaches to SEL interventions. The first approach is the mental health professional as the interventionist. In this model, the counselor or school psychologist enters a classroom to deliver a fifteen- to twenty-minute SEL lesson. That model is certainly better than no intervention at all, but it tends to lack effectiveness. The second model is the classroom teacher as the interventionist. This model is more effective because it is scalable: Each student has the opportunity to receive a lesson on any given day by any given teacher. The third option is the most effective, and that is every adult as the intervention. Note that the intervention in the third model is not a curriculum, per se, but every adult committed to being a living example of emotional intelligence.

> "Since SEL is clearly important, the question then becomes how we empower educators and students with the SEL skill set they will need to be successful."

As we considered the question of how, two key words that guided us were "think systemically." The traditional leader who drives change from the top often creates change-resistant organizations by failing to tap the leadership capacities of the people at all levels within the organization. This means that effective SEL interventions cannot be understood as something only a handful of people are qualified or required to implement. Rather, effective SEL interventions are a commitment made by everyone on a campus or in a district—all leaders and all followers—to be living examples of increasing emotional intelligence. What is true of academic content is also true of SEL: I can't teach what I don't know.

Before I end the chapter, let me go back and address IQ Test Item #4. I left the item unanswered, and I know that will cause many of you teacher types to lose sleep until you find resolution. Okay, here's the deal: I don't know that there is a right answer. I created items that were as random as I could possibly imagine, that bear no real relationship with one another. If we thought long enough about it, we could probably make arguments for any one of the five options. Maybe, if we found someone with an IQ of a bazillion, they would find the answer immediately, but it's not likely. The only thing we can do with a problem like that is to engage our problem-solving skills and make our best guess. We may face the disappointment of not choosing correctly in the end, but we can find peace in the fact that we have done our best with what we were given.

That's probably not the most satisfying answer you'd hope for, but there is a point to it. Sometimes life throws curveballs. I mean, *insane* curveballs. Like a student coming to school with loaded weapons, intent on taking lives. Like a young child living her last few days before finally succumbing to cancer. If you think having a Ph.D. in psychology somehow empowers you with the emotional intelligence to know how to solve (or at least effectively help) those kinds of life problems, I humbly suggest that you are wrong. Sometimes life presents emotional problems

> "Sometimes life throws curveballs. I mean, insane curveballs. Like a student coming to school with loaded weapons, intent on taking lives. Like a young child living her last few days before succumbing to cancer."

that either seem unsolvable or, in fact, are not solvable. When life presents those kinds of problems, our solace comes from doing our best possible work in the approach. What more can we ask of ourselves?

Chapter 1: The Down and Dirty

- Social and emotional learning is essential to responding adaptively (or responding well) to crisis.

- Those who experience long and satisfying careers in education are individuals who are emotionally intelligent. They are known as Life Givers. Educators who don't practice emotional intelligence tend to be miserable and make those around them miserable. They are Life Suckers.

- Social and emotional learning has been validated by research as much as any other academic or behavioral intervention in education. SEL has proved to enhance both academic and behavioral growth in students.

- Educators who are emotionally intelligent are more adaptive, sustainable, and healthy, and they tend to connect more fluidly with their students.

- The most effective teachers of SEL skills are adults who regularly practice the skills themselves.

Chapter 1: SEL in Real Time

1. Consider your day today, in the context of the five elements of SEL (self-awareness, self-regulation, social awareness, social/relationship skills, and responsible decision-making). Name a point in your day when you practiced one of these. Where might there have been a missed opportunity to practice another SEL skill?

2. Think about a recent conversation or email exchange with a colleague, friend, or family member that elicited (in you) an emotional response. Can you identify what emotion was aroused, and how you managed that emotion? See, look at your well-versed SEL-self in the works!

3. Can you think of someone (if you are a teacher, try to think of a particular student) who exhibits a noticeable amount of one of the SEL tenets? Can you think of someone who would benefit from more instruction/practice in one of the SEL skills?

CHAPTER 2

How Can We Know Ourselves?

Until you make the unconscious conscious,
it will direct your life, and you will call it fate.

—Carl Jung, author of *Psychological Types*

Adam and Eve were alone in the garden. They were naked, and they felt no shame. Now, the serpent was more crafty than any of the wild animals the Lord God made. He said to the woman, "Did God really say, 'You must not eat from any tree in the garden'?"

The woman said to the serpent, "We may eat fruit from the trees in the garden, but God did say, 'You must not eat fruit from the tree that is in the middle of the garden, and you must not touch it, or you will die.'"

"You will not certainly die," the serpent said to the woman.

"For God knows that when you eat from it your eyes will be opened, and you will be like God, knowing good and evil."

When the woman saw that the fruit of the tree was good for food and pleasing to the eye, and also desirable for gaining wisdom, she took some and ate it. She also gave some to her husband, who was with her, and he ate it. Then the eyes of both of them were opened, and they realized they were naked; so they sewed fig leaves together and made coverings for themselves. Then the man and his wife heard the sound of the Lord God as he was walking in the garden in the cool of the day, and they hid from the Lord God among the trees of the garden.

But the Lord God called to the man, "Where are you?"

He answered, "I heard you in the garden, and I was afraid because I was naked, so I hid."

—Genesis 2:25–3:10

My training as a theologian and a psychologist leads me to interpret dreams—both mine and those of my clients in clinical practice. Admittedly, interpreting dreams is much more art than science, but generally speaking, certain kinds of dreams can represent deeply embedded hopes and fears. For example, being naked often reveals a deep fear of being exposed.

In the Hebrew text cited above, Adam and Eve were naked, and they felt no shame. What could possibly represent paradise more than being able to be completely vulnerable with no sense of shame? I present me—warts and all—and I get total acceptance. Paradise. After Adam and Eve eat the forbidden fruit, though, God's presence evokes in Adam both an emotion and a subsequent behavior: *"I was afraid because I was naked, and I hid."*

The story of Adam and Eve in the garden illustrates a reality that seems to be universal to the human experience: the fear of our true mental or emotional state being exposed. Just as Adam and Eve responded in shame by covering their nakedness with fig leaves, our fear of being psychologically exposed leads us to cover ourselves with modern-day fig leaves: education, houses, vehicles, designer clothes, intelligence, competence, and achievement. The list could go on to include anything I think I need to add to myself to be deemed worthy, acceptable, admired, good enough, smart enough, competent enough, attractive enough. Just about all of us do it—even the truly rich and famous. "I can imagine looking at [me] and thinking, 'Well, he wouldn't have any insecurities,' but it's not true," Paul McCartney said himself in a *60 Minutes* interview. Knowing oneself can be a daunting endeavor. What if you don't like what you discover?

As I noted in Chapter 1, the most-effective SEL outcomes are seen by the systems in which all adults on campus are not just interventionist, but the intervention (meaning they actually live and model SEL moment-by-moment throughout the school day). There are a couple of key points that we can reflect on to give us courage and motivation to move forward and become living interventions. The first is that whatever ugliness I may find in me is not just in *me*. We all have a shadow. No one has it all together, and everyone has things they don't like about themselves. Fears and insecurities vary from person to person, but their presence is consistent. So, we can take heart because we are all in the same boat. The second key point is that I wield the most power and potential to do the most good in life

> "We all have a shadow. No one has it all together, and everyone has things they don't like about themselves."

> "I wield the most power and potential to do the most good in life when I am most authentic."

when I am most authentic. The honest, flawed me has more inherent credibility than the polished, fake me. That's great news, because it means I have no need to hide behind the illusion of the perfect physique, the perfect marriage, the perfect children, the perfect professional evaluation, the perfect whatever. I can imagine we'd all agree that we're far from perfect, but the harder question to answer is: Who are we? What are we naturally good at, and what are we not?

Psychologists Joseph Luft and Harrison Ingham developed a tech-nique to help people get to know themselves, the Johari Window.

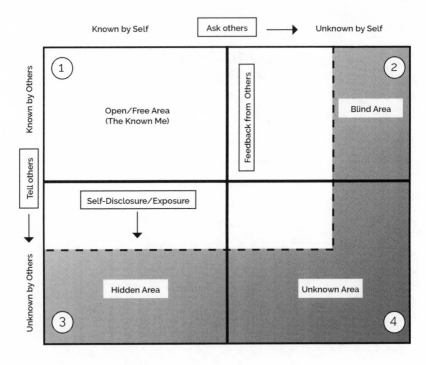

Figure 2: The Johari Window

As you can see, we increase what we know about ourselves in two ways: by self-disclosure and exposure, and by asking for feedback from others. While these seem scary, and very well could deliver answers that are hard to swallow, they are crucial if we want to grow in authenticity.

If we avoid the difficult task of self-exploration, we limit our Open/Free Area, and become the individual who is not self-aware. These are people who micromanage, nothing is ever their fault, they make excuses or rationalize their shortcomings and failures, they are defensive when confronted, they commonly say things that are offensive or off-putting to others, they lack the ability to laugh at themselves, and they bully. These defense mechanisms are employed to either distract from dealing with—or to hide—the real self. Do you think people who do these things are agents for positive change? No. They are too busy protecting or defending themselves to truly love and care for others.

Once we embrace the compelling reasons to increase our self-awareness, how do we actually do it? In our EQ-uipped Classroom workshops, we invite educators to explore three essential domains in which to practice self-awareness: knowing emotions (my internal weather), knowing personality type (my internal climate), and knowing stress (my external storms). Let's start with knowing emotions.

The Weather: My Emotions

We use the word "heart" in association with emotion: "My ex-girlfriend broke my heart when she voted for the wrong presidential candidate." Technically, though, she broke your brain—the limbic system, to be exact, which is where emotion lives. A main component of the limbic system is the amygdala, which is named from the Latin *amugdalē* (almond). The amygdala is an almond-shaped mass of gray matter located deep within the temporal lobes of the brain that performs a primary role in the processing of memory and emotional responses—including fear, anxiety, and aggression.

Emotions give us information about the world around us to help us become more adaptive by either speeding up or slowing down. Though we don't have a clear answer about how many core emotions are contained within the human experience, we do know that an essential role of emotions is to activate the autonomic nervous system (either the sympathetic nervous system or the parasympathetic nervous system) to arouse or soothe us.

Activation of the sympathetic nervous system is about arousal, and it is often referred to as the fight-or-flight system. When this system is activated, the pupils dilate (I need more light to see what's going on around me), the heart rate and respiration rate increase (I'll need more oxygen to fight or run, and I'll need more blood to circulate the oxygen), perspiration increases (I'll need to sweat to cool my body), and the stress hormones adrenaline and cortisol are produced (I'll need increased energy to fuel all these responses).

Activation of the parasympathetic nervous system is about soothing, and it is often referred to as the "rest and digest" system. Upon activation, the pupils constrict (I need less light so I can initiate sleep), salivation increases (so I can digest my food), respiration and heart rate decrease (so my body can initiate a state of rest), and digestive enzymes are produced (so I can digest and store food). We'll discuss this more in the next chapter, but the concepts of arousal and soothing are critical points in understanding how to regulate ourselves.

When we developed the EASEL, we wanted to include a domain that measured someone's capacity to recognize their own emotion. Sample items from this domain include the following:

- "I think about the causes of my emotions."

- "I experience very few emotional highs and lows."

The resulting score on the Recognition of Self scale (which measures the degree to which someone can accurately recognize their own thoughts, feelings, strengths, and weaknesses) provides valuable insight about possibilities for growth. Key components of self-recognition include being able to notice the wide spectrum of emotion (emotional valence), the intensity of emotion (emotional

> "Since much of our behavior is emotion-driven, not knowing our emotions means not knowing why we do and don't do certain things."

arousal), and being able to track one's thoughts (meta-awareness). Individuals who score high in this domain have been described as reflective, self-aware, self-confident, and insightful. Individuals who fall in the low range have been described as emotionally flat or reserved, and might be perceived as aloof and standoffish. A low score on this scale may signal that one displays emotions inappropriately (because they are unaware of them) and is blind to the emotions of others (because they cannot identify them in themselves).

Since much of our behavior is emotion-driven, not knowing our emotions means not knowing why we do and don't do certain things. As Socrates famously noted: "The unexamined life is not worth living." Also, one becomes at risk for physical illness

"To help keep tabs on their emotional life, I encourage teachers I consult with to ask themselves these kinds of questions on a daily basis: How does this parent make me feel? How does this coworker make me feel? How does this administrator make me feel? How does this student make me feel? Do those feelings arouse me or soothe me?"

when intense emotion goes unidentified and unexpressed over time.

To help keep tabs on their emotional lives, I encourage teachers I consult with to ask themselves these kinds of questions on a daily basis: How does this parent make me feel? How does this coworker make me feel? How does this administrator make me feel? How does this student make me feel? Do those feelings arouse me or soothe me?

The Climate: My Personality

We can think of emotions as weather, which can change day-to-day and potentially moment-to-moment. Personality, though, is more like climate, which tends to be more stable and predictable over time. If you're searching for a test to measure your personality, you'll have no problem finding options—just do a basic internet search for "online personality test." The most commonly known are the MMPI-2, the DISC, and the Enneagram, but you'll find tests that associate your personality with colors, animals, and seasons of the year.

Some of those tests are fun to take and can lead to interesting follow-up conversations, but many (if not most) do not have adequate psychometric properties. In other words, we don't know for sure that people who the tests determine are otters (or purples or winters) really are otters across time, or if they are otters when compared to otters who have been proven to be otters (or purples, winters, etc.).

Among personality tests, the Big 5 Model (also called the Five Factor Model) of personality is the most empirically validated approach, meaning that the five personality constructs that the instrument measures have been replicated across populations, instruments, and time. We can feel good about using it, and that's why we've incorporated the Big 5 assessment into the EASEL. When teachers and administrators using our curriculum take the EASEL, the resulting report lets them know which of the five personality factors emerged as the strongest. These are the five main factors, with their associated strengths and weaknesses:

Personality Dimension #1: Openness

The Openness to Experience scale measures the degree of intellectual curiosity, creativity, and preference for change that one demonstrates. Individuals who score high on this scale have been described as adventurous, imaginative, and entrepreneurial. Those who score low on this scale have been described as liking predictability and being slow to change.

Openness at Best

- **[High Score]** Thinking creatively, outside conventional boundaries; exploring and discovering; creatively allocating resources; adjusting well to change.

  o **Example:** *"Robert is such a creative thinker. He always has a unique perspective for problem solving, and he's willing to try anything at least once."*

- **[Low Score]** Consistency, predictability, and reliability; invoking trust from others because of dependability; strong loyalty; paying attention to detail.

  o **Example:** *"Amy has served in every capacity in her community organization for over seventeen years; everyone knows she's the backbone of that agency."*

Openness at Worst

- **[High Score]** Losing the benefits of consistency and pattern; introducing change too frequently, suddenly, or drastically at the unnecessary expense of others.

  o **Example:** *"We just got the new system up and running when Robert decided to launch the new latest-and-greatest system. We'll never keep up, and everyone is getting pretty discouraged."*

- **[Low Score]** Getting stuck in a rut and missing out on opportunity; losing capacity to motivate or excite others.

  o **Example:** *"I hear Amy still records her favorite shows on VHS cassettes. No, seriously."*

Personality Dimension #2: Conscientiousness

The Conscientiousness scale measures the individual's propensity to display self-discipline and to be known for dutiful achievement. Individuals who score high on this scale have been described as orderly and exacting, often achieving against all odds. Those who score low on this scale have been described as carefree and fun-loving.

Conscientiousness at Best

- **[High Score]** Focused, organized, and able to see projects through to completion; disciplined and dependable; task oriented.

  o Example: *"Adam has lists for his lists. If it's on his list, you can count on it getting done. He's the epitome of the old saying, 'If you want something to get done, give it to someone who's busy.'"*

- **[Low Score]** Flexible, spontaneous, comfortable with disorder; good at multi-tasking.

  o Example: *"LaTonya loves a loud class—it looks like chaos, but you'll never believe how much those kids are learning!"*

Conscientiousness at Worst

- **[High Score]** Valuing the completion of tasks over the quality of relationships; potentially stubborn, overly demanding, or obsessive.

  o Example: *"If you don't get on Adam's list, he won't know you exist. And even if he does know, you may not think he cares."*

- **[Low Score]** Excessively casual, inconsistent, irresponsible, or disorganized; cannot be trusted with leadership tasks.

  o Example: *"Everyone loves LaTonya, but paperwork? Forget about it—it will be in the last minute of the last day possible."*

Personality Dimension #3: Extraversion

The Extraversion scale measures presence of personality traits such as positive emotions, assertiveness, sociability, and the tendency to seek and enjoy the company of others. Individuals who score high on this scale have been described as outgoing, friendly, and easy to get along with. Extraverts are energized in groups. Individuals who score low on this scale have been described as reserved, serious, and avoiding leadership roles. Introverts are energized in solitude.

Extraversion at Best

- **[High Score]** Thriving in large groups and loud, busy spaces; may emerge as a natural leader in group situations.

    o **Example:** *"Angela knows everyone! She made the coolest plan for everyone to take a trip together! Miss Congeniality."*

- **[Low Score]** High threshold for being alone; potentially reflective and insightful.

    o **Example:** *"Thad could go for days without talking to a soul. He's like a monk on a retreat. He's so at peace with himself."*

Extraversion at Worst

- **[High Score]** Too outspoken, aggressive, or shallow; may lack self-awareness and may be prone to dominate a conversation.

    o **Example:** *"Angela is the life of the party, but sometimes it feels like I'm just an extra in the Angela Show. It gets old."*

- **[Low Score]** Aloof, withdrawn, and uncaring; may demonstrate poor social skills due to preference for being alone; may not be ideally suited for leadership positions due to difficulty engaging effectively with others.

  o **Example:** *"Thad's classes are the quietest classes I've ever been in. I learned a lot, but I'm not sure I'd ever feel comfortable going to his office hours. I think he'd just sit and stare at me."*

Personality Dimension #4: Agreeableness

The Agreeableness scale measures the presence of personality traits that include compassion and innate trust of others. Individuals who score high on this scale have been described as eager to please and as valuing cooperation over competition. Those who score low on this scale have been described as competitive, challenging, and prone to argument.

Agreeableness at Best

- **[High Score]** Relating to authority by being tolerant, humble, and accommodating; being emotionally accessible and having a high capacity to build relationships with people who are different than them; being a good team player.

  o **Example:** *"Kristen is the definition of kindness: Seriously—everyone loves her—from the cool girls to the really weird ones!"*

- **[Low Score]** Persistent, competitive, and independent; having a questioning skepticism that keeps others honest; capable of setting boundaries with others.

  o Example: *"Shelly plays to win—whether it's a board game or a philosophical argument. She keeps you on your toes!"*

Agreeableness at Worst

- **[High Score]** Too highly accommodating at times when boundaries need to be set; people-pleasing; being averse to conflict and difficult conversations.

  o Example: *"Kristen hasn't asked for a raise even though she totally deserves one. I think she's depressed and frustrated because her work is being taken for granted."*

- **[Low Score]** Being brash, abrasive, and aggressive; valuing ideas and winning over relational peace and well-being; being self-centered and combative.

  o Example: *"Shelly wants to be the best at everything. She thinks everything is a competition—it's rude and exhausting. It can make it hard to be friends with her."*

Personality Dimension #5: Neuroticism

The Neuroticism scale measures the tendency to be prone to psychological stress and to experience unpleasant emotions easily. Individuals who score high on this scale have been described as worriers who are prone to unusually high emotional vacillation. Those who score low on this scale have been described as able to manage stressful situations without emotional arousal and as being emotionally resilient.

Neuroticism at Best

- **[High Score]** Alert, mindful of surroundings, and rarely caught off guard; potentially able to thrive in chaotic energy; concerned and attentive when needs arise.

  ○ **Example:** *"Carol's middle name should be 'Constant Vigilance'! She's always on the lookout—she reads all the reviews, she gets her flu shot, she gets her keys out of her purse before she gets to the parking lot. She can really save your bacon because she's already foreseen a problem and solved it for you!"*

- **[Low Score]** In control, secure, stress free.

  ○ **Example:** *"Rusty is the definition of 'even-keel'—he's totally unflappable. You could have the most disgusting growth on your foot, and he'd still look at it unfazed and say, 'Huh. Looks like you've got something there.' Just like the sky is blue and today is Tuesday."*

Neuroticism at Worst

- **[High Score]** May overcommit or behave controllingly due to hyper-arousal/hyper-vigilance; prone to physical illness due to chronic worry and anxiety; emotional instability.

  ○ **Example:** *"Carol is making herself crazy trying to figure out all the things to worry about with moving offices. Most of them are not even possible, but she's freaking out."*

Personality Trait	Low Score: Below 2	Middle Score: 2–4	High Score: Above 4
Openness The degree to which we are open to new experiences and new ways of doing things	**Preserver** Consistency, predictability, and reliability; invoking trust from others because of dependability; loyal; paying attention to detail	**Moderate** Can appreciate both innovation and efficiency, but neither in the extreme	**Progressive** Thinking creatively, outside conventional boundaries; exploring and discovering; adjusting well to change
Conscientiousness The degree to which we focus on tasks and push toward goals	**Flexible** Spontaneous, comfortable with disorder; good at multi-tasking	**Balanced** Able to balance getting things done while taking good care of self; capable of being parallel and linear	**Firm** Organized, and able to see projects through to completion; disciplined and dependable; task oriented
Extraversion The degree to which we tolerate sensory stimulation from other people and situations	**Introvert** High threshold for being alone; potentially reflective and insightful	**Ambivert** Able to shift between working alone and working with groups; bored if in one extreme or the other for too long	**Extravert** Thriving in large groups and loud, busy spaces; may emerge as a natural leader in group situations
Agreeableness The degree to which we focus on relationships and defer to others	**Challenger** Competitive and independent; having a questioning skepticism that keeps others honest; capable of setting boundaries with others	**Negotiator** Able to shift between competitive and cooperative modes fluidly; most capable of finding win-win; neither dependent nor independent	**Adapter** Relates to authority by being tolerant, humble, and accommodating; able to build relationships across differences; good team player
Neuroticism The degree to which we respond to stress and other emotional stimuli	**Resilient** In control; secure; unmoved by stress	**Responsive** Normally calm, but surprises can lead to discouragement or anxiety; may need a moment to collect self after crisis before moving to problem-solving mode	**Reactive** Alert, mindful of surroundings, and rarely caught off guard; concerned and attentive when needs arise

Figure 3: Summary of EASEL Big-5 Personality Traits: Me at My Best

Personality Trait	Low Score: Below 2	Middle Score: 2–4	High Score: Above 4
Openness The degree to which we are open to new experiences and new ways of doing things	**Preserver** Getting stuck in a rut and missing out on opportunity; losing capacity to motivate or excite others	**Moderate** Failing to change or failing to remain consistent due to discomfort with either extreme; may be perceived as too middle-of-the-road/ non-committal	**Progressive** Losing the benefits of consistency and pattern; introducing change too frequently at the unnecessary expense of others
Conscientiousness The degree to which we focus on tasks and push toward goals	**Flexible** Excessively casual, inconsistent, irresponsible, or disorganized; cannot be trusted with leadership tasks	**Balanced** Inability to complete a task that requires intensive focus; inability to multi-task in chaotic environments	**Firm** Valuing the completion of tasks over the quality of relationships; potentially stubborn, overly demanding, or obsessive
Extraversion The degree to which we tolerate sensory stimulation from other people and situations	**Introvert** Aloof, withdrawn, and uncaring; may not be ideal for leadership positions due to difficulty engaging effectively with others	**Ambivert** May be perceived by extraverts as an introvert; may be perceived by introverts as an extravert	**Extravert** Too outspoken, aggressive, or shallow; may lack self-awareness and may be prone to dominate a conversation
Agreeableness The degree to which we focus on relationships and defer to others	**Challenger** Being brash, abrasive, and aggressive; valuing ideas and winning over relational well-being; being self-centered and combative	**Negotiator** May be regarded as sitting on the fence between two sides	**Adapter** Too highly accommodating when boundaries need to be set; people-pleasing; being averse to conflict and difficult conversations
Neuroticism The degree to which we respond to stress and other emotional stimuli	**Resilient** May be perceived as lacking in concern or empathy; may not take serious situations with the gravity they warrant	**Responsive** May be perceived as reactive by the resilient, and as apathetic by the reactive	**Reactive** May overcommit or overcontrol due to hyper-arousal/hyper-vigilance; prone to physical illness due to chronic worry and anxiety

Figure 4: Summary of EASEL Big-5 Personality Traits: Me at My Worst

- **[Low Score]** May be perceived as lacking in concern or empathy; inability to respond in a timely manner; may not take serious situations with the gravity they warrant.

  ○ **Example:** *"Rusty just told me his dad is really sick. It was weird—he was so matter-of-fact about it, and I know that he and his dad are super close."*

As you can see, considering our personality in light of these five factors gives us a taste of what it means to know ourselves. The strengths and weaknesses associated with each provide valuable information about how to function most effectively when working with anyone. So, my emotions (the weather) are the first thing I need to be aware of and my personality (the climate) is the second thing. Let's move on to the third and final arena of self-awareness: the storms outside.

> "Effectively managing stress is essential to our sustainability, and effective stress management begins with identifying how vulnerable we are to experiencing stress."

The Storms: My Stress

Stress is energy our bodies produce when we wonder whether we deal effectively with a given situation. For practical purposes, stress is essentially fear and anxiety. Thinking back to the internal weather of our emotions, we know that emotions will activate either the sympathetic or parasympathetic nervous systems. Since stress is fear, it activates our sympathetic nervous system to arouse us to fight or flight. Physical indications that we are experiencing stress and that our body is producing energy include increased heart rate, shallow or rapid breathing, muscle tension, and perspiration.

This energy—the neurochemical cocktail our bodies create—is intended to serve as fuel that will power us to either fight or run from what is scaring us. Stress energy can be good, as it is often a key ingredient in peak performance. However, if we are too stressed for too long, the chronic presence of these chemicals can have devastating effects on our emotions, our immune system, the clarity of our cognitive processes, and our digestive system. As you might imagine, then, effectively managing stress is essential to our sustainability, and effective stress management begins with identifying how vulnerable we are to experiencing stress.

When we review EASEL results with educators in our workshops, we pay special attention to the Optimism, Tolerance, and Flexibility scales, as high scores on those scales are positively correlated with resilience to stress. If you score high on the Neuroticism personality scale and low on the Optimism, Tolerance, and Flexibility scales, you are a stress ball waiting to explode (honestly, it probably already did happen). In contrast, if you score high on the Agreeableness personality scale and high on the Optimism, Tolerance, and Flexibility scales, you carry much more innate resilience to stress.

Figure 5: Three Arenas of Self-Awareness

Andrea's Journey Into Self-Awareness

Andrea's first session with me was triggered by her five-year itch. She was in her late twenties and had just started her fifth year of teaching. Andrea was intelligent and insightful, and my educated guess is that she had the potential to be successful in any number of vocations. But the way she was feeling at the time put her at a crossroads: *Is this really what I want to do with the rest of my life?*

We settled into the first session with the usual procedures. She signed a few forms and I reviewed limits of confidentiality.

"You actually came and presented to our district," Andrea said with a chuckle. "It was on 'The Power of a Teacher' and you talked about the importance of caring for ourselves. I remember thinking: *'I wonder if this guy could help me.'*"

I chuckled with her. "I hope I can help. Tell me a little about what's going on."

"I don't even know where to begin. I guess I'm just totally overwhelmed at work," she explained. "This is my fifth year, and I'm just not sure I can go on."

She went on to describe stressors and headaches that almost anyone in education, certainly classroom teachers, could relate to: increased demands for students to perform on standardized tests, increased paperwork, longer hours, a shifting student demographic, and teacher turnover. She expressed a genuine love for all of her students, including the ones who absorbed disproportionately large amounts of her time and energy.

Beyond the stressors of work, Andrea was a young woman attempting to separate herself from her dysfunctional family: "My family was crazy. I mean like actual batshit crazy. Every day it seemed like someone was always going off on someone else about whatever. I mean, it was insane. At some point I learned to shut off my feelings just to deal with it."

As a general rule, repressing emotion is recipe for both physical and psychological dysfunction. I could see the heaviness in her face and on her shoulders as she spoke. She was literally slumped in her chair by the end of the session.

"You're going through so much, Andrea. I can definitely see why you're feeling overwhelmed," I offered in conclusion. I felt sad. I sensed that in her heart (actually, it was in her amygdala, wasn't it?), she wanted to do what was right. She wanted to be a voice and light for children. How devastating to wonder whether any good you hope to do in the world will be precluded by variables beyond your control.

"Thank you so much for letting me into your world," I said. "You've named several things at work that aren't going well, and I feel like I have a good overview. Let's schedule again for next week, and when you come back, I want you to be prepared to discuss just one thing. Between now and then, you choose the one issue at work you'd like to address, and I'll bet we can get you on the right track."

Andrea came the next week, seeming even more determined this time.

"I want to talk about relationships," she jumped in straight away. She was sitting erect, upright. "Two in particular: the girl I co-teach with and my principal."

"Okay, great," I said with a smile. I appreciated the energy in her voice. "Let's start with your co-teacher. Tell me about her."

"Well, she tries to be sweet. She really does," Andrea explained. "But I'm so sick of her giving me advice when I don't need it. She treats me the way my mother treats me, but she's only three years older than me, and she's only been teaching one year more than me."

"How do you feel when you're around your mother?" I asked.

"I don't know," Andrea answered slowly. "I've never really thought about it."

"Take your time," I reassured her.

"She's so condescending," she answered in a sudden burst of energy. "I feel condescended to, and it pisses me off. It's like my mom refuses to let go of some twelve-year-old version of me. I think it's so she'll always feel like she's needed or something."

Wow. Was there ever so much to unpack in that answer!

"Okay, now tell me about your principal," I continued.

Andrea chuckled. "She's like twenty or thirty years older than me, but she has no ability to set boundaries or confront people when they need to be confronted. It drives me crazy! I just want her to lead, for crying out loud, but she's so concerned with being nice to everyone that I think she's afraid she's going to hurt their feelings. She reminds me so much of my sister!"

"And how do you feel when you're around your sister?" I asked.

She laughed out loud, beginning to connect the dots. "Oh my god, my sister drives me crazy! She is such a people pleaser, and she ends up dating loser guys who treat her like crap because she can't set boundaries and she has no self-respect."

"Okay," I responded, "but name a feeling."

She paused for a moment. "Disgust. I feel disgust, and I have no respect for her."

"So," I summarized, "two of the adults that are most relevant to your day-to-day functioning remind you of people you are trying to get away from, and they make you feel condescended to and disgusted?"

Andrea paused again. "You know, I hadn't really thought of it that specifically, but yes. I feel like I spend a good part of my day swimming in those two feelings. Great. I come to therapy and discover that I'm working with my mother and sister."

"No wonder you want to leave," I offered with a half-smile. "I probably would, too. But I want you to know that you are doing an incredibly noble work on your campus, and you don't have to leave it just because of the way people make you feel. We can find ways to help you direct the emotions rather than repress them or carry them around inside you. In fact, believe it or not, we can learn to understand those emotions as dashboard lights that are giving us information about the engine of our internal world. Those very emotions can propel you to greater success with your students and to greater relational harmony not just with your co-teacher and principal, but with your sister and mother as well."

She sat in silence for a moment. "I'm all in," she finally offered, with conviction. "But how?"

My Journey Into Self-Awareness

It wasn't until I was working on my master's degree in counseling that I admitted I needed help. I was getting by in my work as a case manager for a foster placement agency, but I was finding that working with children who have experienced trauma was taking a toll on me. I was becoming increasingly disengaged in a way that was not good for me, or the foster children and families I was serving. I was having trouble sleeping, and I found myself struggling to complete my academic load. It wasn't just work. It was my personal life too. My wife, Kim, and I had been dating for about a year at that point, and the conversations we were beginning to

have about marriage were giving me panic attacks (but don't tell
her I admitted to that). I picked up and then hung up the phone
four times before I actually had the courage to dial the number to
schedule my first therapy session. I had never told anyone about
the trauma I experienced, either, and now in my late twenties,
I was realizing that certain events still held a death grip on my
mind and heart.

I was so nervous before my first session that I almost threw up
in the parking lot of my therapist's office. I walked into the office,
signed a few forms, sat, and waited. A few moments later, a soft-
spoken gentleman with deep kindness in his face opened the door
and introduced himself.

"Good afternoon, Adam. My name is Dr. Steve Smith, but
most people just call me Dr. Steve," he said. With a handshake,
Dr. Steve invited me back to his office.

"So, what brings you in today, Adam?" Dr. Steve asked after a
short pause.

I hesitated. "I'm not sure," I lied. I knew exactly what brought
me in. My eyes locked into a distant gaze out the window. I could
not stop my right knee from bouncing—"psychomotor agitation,"
we call it in technical jargon.

Dr. Steve sensed my tension. "Many patients feel nervous or
anxious during the first few moments of their first session," he
offered. "It can be a scary experience, especially when you're not
sure what to expect." I nodded, my eyes still focused outside.

After a few minutes of small talk—traffic, weather, sports—
Dr. Steve patiently asked, "So, how can I help you?"

I could tell that he both sincerely wanted to know and help,
and that absolutely terrified me. I had no clue where to begin.
Houston? The Valley? My first arrest? The sexual assault? My

friends' deaths? My ongoing depression? My deep-seated sense of inadequacy? My crippling fear of vulnerability and emotional intimacy?

I found myself resisting the process, and I resented him for pressing in. I felt like a five-year-old boy on an examination table scrambling from a doctor who was trying to stab me with a malaria vaccination. My eyes finally shifted from the window, and I looked at him. Dr. Steve asked a few more questions, but I didn't respond. I just locked up. The remainder of our session was a forty-three-minute staring contest. There were a few deep sighs, a few shifts in posture, but not another word was spoken. I distinctly remember the sound of the clock's pendulum clicking . . . away . . . every . . . second . . . of . . . each . . . passing . . . minute.

When the clock reached ten minutes to the hour, Dr. Steve concluded the session. "Adam," he said, shifting forward in his seat, "I can only be as helpful to you as you are able to be honest with me and yourself. You are here for a reason, and I'd like to help you." He paused, as if to let his words sink in. "Would you like to schedule another appointment now, or do you want to think about it and maybe get back to me later?"

Every fiber in my being wanted to run. I took a deep breath, still staring out the window. "Can we meet again at this time next week?" I asked, immediately wishing I could take it back.

"Absolutely," he said. "I'll look forward to it."

I spent the next six days terrified at the thought of another fifty minutes in Dr. Steve's office. I had buyer's remorse: What was the point of going back to therapy? Were we just going to stare at each other for another fifty minutes? Maybe my life wasn't that bad after all, and I should just move on.

Exactly one week after the staring contest, I arrived at Dr.

Steve's office, still uncomfortable, but not quite throwing-up-in-the-parking-lot scared. I entered his office, and the session started off benignly enough with five minutes of small talk: "Did the Spurs win last night? No, but I'm not too worried about it. They usually have a mid-season slump before making a good playoff run." After a short lull, Dr. Steve said, "It's good to see you again, Adam. I'm truly glad you came back."

I smiled. "I know why I'm here," I said.

Dr. Steve returned a reassuring smile and nodded.

There was a moment of silence, and then, seemingly out of nowhere, it happened. It was the weirdest thing: I simply came undone. I heaved a cry so heavy, so deep, and so filled with pain that I honestly thought I was going to pass out. There seemed to be no end to it—this ugly cry, this guttural wailing; just as it would begin to subside, it would start all over again, a raging thunderstorm of years of unexpressed emotion.

Through the deep, heaving sobs, I managed only ten words that entire second session: "Things happened to me that I've never told anyone about."

Dr. Steve was incredibly patient and empathetic. Twice during the session, he asked gently probing questions: Did it have to do with my family? Was I hurt in some way? I couldn't respond, other than to hold up my trembling right hand and shake my head "No," meaning, "I can't go any further."

Looking back, I realize now that my problem wasn't an inability

"I would learn, also later in the process, that my personality type would be a huge asset in my recovery, and that as my personality shifted through my healing, my vulnerability to stress would increase."

to identify my emotions. That actually became a problem later on in the process, as I learned to nuance emotion, but for now, it certainly wasn't the presenting problem. I knew full well why I was in his office: I was overwhelmed with feelings of anger and sadness about my childhood. I would come to learn that my personality type would be a huge asset in my recovery, and that as my personality shifted through my healing, my vulnerability to stress would increase. My problem, as I would learn in session three, was that even though I could recognize my emotions, I was not skilled in regulating them.

Chapter 2: The Down and Dirty

- Vulnerability (opening up to others) can be scary. It is only when we are honest with ourselves and with others, though, that we can truly grow and minimize our blind spots and biases.

- Self-awareness begins with being able to identify our emotions. They originate in our brain, not our heart, and serve to either speed us up (fight or flight) or slow us down (rest and digest).

- In addition to being aware of our emotions, we also need to be aware of our personality type. The EASEL identifies five personality traits: Openness to New Experience, Conscientiousness, Extraversion, Agreeableness, and Neuroticism. Everyone possesses these five traits in varying proportions, and there are strengths and weaknesses associated with scoring high and low on each of the five scales.

- A therapy client of mine, Andrea, learned to identify intense emotions she was experiencing at work as a teacher: disgust and feeling condescended to.

- I almost threw up before my first therapy session. Once I got there, I sat in silence for almost the entire hour.

Chapter 2: SEL in Real Time

Welcome to *Personality Jeopardy!*, where we will become more familiar with the Big 5 personality traits and identifying markers of each of them. Your objective is to identify which trait is being described, and whether the person is high or low in that trait. If playing alone, simply read the description and make your best guess before checking the Answer Key. If playing with a group, choose who will be Alex Trebek and as soon as a group member has an answer, tap your figurative buzzer (this can be any spot you choose, e.g., the edge of the table). Be sure to keep score, so the ones low on Agreeableness will be more motivated to participate.

To review, the traits are:

- Neuroticism

- Openness to Experience

- Conscientiousness

- Extraversion

- Agreeableness

Neuroticism

Descriptions:

1. Sarah's most trusted companion is her hand sanitizer. She carries three different forms of it in her purse and must douse the restaurant table and bench before sitting—not to mention those sticky, smudgy menus.

2. Around the holidays, Uncle Mike would often retreat to the bathroom just to grab a breather alone. So many people in such a crowded room, all loudly engaging with each other, was not his safe space.

3. Jay owns a clothing store downtown that really serves as an outpost for those who need someone to talk to. He hosts all kinds of events there, from concerts to free dinners for the homeless. Even though he posts the business hours on the door, folks are welcomed like family no matter the time.

4. Jen gets her oil changed every 3,000 miles and her hair cut every four weeks. She completes her taxes by January 15 each year and arrives early to church every Sunday.

5. Matt and his wife traveled the continent out of an ambulance he converted into a camper. With their three small children in tow, they made it from Florida to Washington and back in two months, stopping at National Parks along the way.

6. Whenever Mom says she'll be by, add an hour or two to that time. It's likely she'll need to stop by the office to drop off some overdue documents and then pop into the grocery store to grab a few things.

Finishing last is not an option in Dante's mind. As an experienced marathoner, he would rather not have competed at all than to suffer the humiliation of having to accept third place.

Answer Key:

1. Sarah: High on Neuroticism scale

2. Uncle Mike: Low on Extraversion scale

3. Jay: High on Agreeableness scale

4. Jen: High on Conscientiousness scale

5. Matt: High on Openness to Experience scale

6. Mom: Low on Conscientiousness scale

7. Dante: Low on Agreeableness scale

CHAPTER 3

How Can We Regulate Ourselves?

Anything that's human is mentionable, and anything that is mentionable can be more manageable. When we can talk about our feelings, they become less overwhelming, less upsetting, and less scary. The people we trust with that important talk can help us know that we are not alone.

—Fred Rogers, television personality and Presbyterian minister

n *The Different Drum: Community Making and Peace*, American psychiatrist M. Scott Peck eloquently describes the emotional environment in his family of origin:

> Each of my parents was responsible and caring. There was plenty of warmth, affection, laughter, and celebration. The only problem was that certain emotions

were unacceptable. My parents had no difficulty being angry . . . [but] never once one in all my years of growing up did I ever hear either of my parents say that they were anxious or worried or scared or depressed or anything to indicate that they felt other than on top of things and in total control of their lives . . . the problem is that I was not free to be me.

Peck would go on to have debilitating anxiety and depression as a young adult because experiencing and appropriately expressing those emotions was not modeled for him in childhood—not the ideal situation. As those of us who have children will attest, though, the ideal situation doesn't always play out in practice, even in the healthiest of families. Our day-to-day lives inevitably communicate spoken and unspoken rules about which emotions are acceptable and unacceptable for experience, and we run the risk of expressing emotions with words and actions that can be harmful to those around us.

In Chapter 2, we explored how we can take that potentially scary first step toward knowing ourselves: naming our feelings, starting to learn our personality, and noticing our vulnerability to stress. It may be that self-awareness feels so intimidating because we're left with the question of what to do with what we find: *What if I'm an irreconcilable mess?* Most people feel this way when they begin this process. The good news is that, regardless of what you and I might find with regard to our emotions,

> "It may be that self-awareness feels so intimidating because we're left with the question of what to do with what we find: What if I'm an irreconcilable mess?"

personality, or vulnerability to stress, there are practical steps we can take to manage and regulate these things.

Managing My Emotions

Let's go back to the amygdala and the electrochemical packets of information we call emotion that activate either the arousal (fight or flight) or soothing (rest and digest) responses. We often hear of emotion as being categorized as either good (e.g., happiness, joy, excitement) or bad (e.g., anger, frustration, confusion). I think we arrived at those descriptors because of the behaviors we often see associated with them. When people do good, helpful things, those behaviors are often fueled by happiness, joy, or excitement, and when people do bad, harmful things, those behaviors are often fueled by anger, frustration, or confusion. The reality, though, is that emotions are neither good nor bad; we can think of them as amoral fuel. For example, I can take a five-gallon tank of gasoline, pour it into my truck, and give you a ride to the grocery store. In that case, the fuel is a blessing. I can take the same five-gallon tank of gas, pour it throughout your house, and burn it down. In that case, the fuel is a curse. In the end, though, it was about how I directed the fuel, and not about the fuel itself. The same is true with emotion: Any emotion can be harnessed as a fuel source to make our lives better and more adaptive.

Remember I mentioned that the neurochemical byproducts of excessive stress could wreak havoc on one's digestive system? I've lived that. I've always been a Type A person (I score extremely high on the Conscientiousness scale). Combine that with a decent dose of anxiety and to say that I tend to take on more than I should is quite an understatement. My working motto up until

> "Any emotion can be harnessed as a fuel source to make our lives better and more adaptive."

recent years had always been "If one of something is good, seventeen of them are not only better, but necessary."

About three years ago, I was serving as the clinical director of an outpatient mental health clinic in College Station. I had just finished my second book and was traveling the country conducting workshops for educators. Meanwhile, my wife and I were parenting four teenagers. I worked out religiously, and I ran a half marathon every December. At some point, I began to notice the presence of physical symptoms after I ate certain foods: joint pain, indigestion, headaches, chronic fatigue, and difficulty sleeping. It got so bad that within the period of three months, I went from being able to run thirteen miles to having an extremely difficult time walking a quarter mile.

After consultation with countless doctors and specialists, my wife, Kim, ended up providing me with the insight I needed to begin to heal. Since she and my son, Andrew, have celiac disease, she has developed an extremely nuanced ability to link physical symptoms to food. At her suggestion, I began an elimination diet and tracked associated physical symptoms. I was both amazed and relieved to find that after a two-week detox of eating nothing but homemade organic vegetable soup, all of my symptoms went away.

- At the time, I was thinking, "Great. I was ill, but now that this detox healed me, I can go back to my normal eating." So, I did, and all the symptoms came right back. The message my body was sending me was clear: "Hey, buddy, you're not getting it. This isn't about a food vacation. You need to completely and indefinitely stop eating dairy, gluten, grains, and processed sugars." This is a partial list of the comfort foods I had to break up with:

- Blue Bell Cookies and Cream ice cream
- Baked potatoes topped with Land-O-Lakes butter, Kraft sharp cheddar cheese, and Daisy sour cream
- Tostitos Hint of Lime tortilla chips
- State Fair corn dogs
- Chick-O-Stick candy (this one really hurt)
- DiGiorno rising crust Hawaiian pizza

The list could go on, but it hurts too much to write. I spent months in denial: "It couldn't have been the small pint of Blue Bell. It must have been the weather." I spent months in anger: "This isn't fair. I work out and try to take good care of my body—except for the really poor stress management piece." I spent months in bargaining: "Maybe if I keep eating homemade organic vegetable soup, I can also eat Hawaiian pizza on the weekend." I also spent months in depression: "It sure sucks to be me." I didn't get to the final stage of grieving—acceptance—until I circled back to anger. I finally learned to access my anger as fuel to make changes in my life. For example, when I felt angry about what I was craving but couldn't eat, I would clean the kitchen to make it an inviting place to cook meals. When I felt angry about going out and watching everyone eat dessert, I would look online for the best anti-inflammatory diets that included foods that were safe for me. When I felt angry about arthritic pain, diarrhea, or headaches, I would prepare foods in the dehydrator.

Looking back, I can say that I'm actually grateful for the anger, because it ended up being an incredibly helpful fuel source to move me forward. As I adjusted to my new normal, my feelings of anger were no longer useful or relevant, and they naturally subsided. Emotions can drive any relationship—with food, family, a spouse, a vocation—for better or worse. Any emotion can be accessed as a fuel source to increase our adaptivity in the world and make our lives better, richer, and more fulfilling.

The EASEL Regulation of Self scale measures the degree to which one appropriately manages their emotions, impulses, and resources, after having identified them (see Recognition of Self scale). Individuals who score in the high range have been described as self-controlled, mature, responsible, conscientious, adaptive, and trustworthy. Those with low scores have been described as impulsive and moody (the proverbial "loose cannon"). To learn where you land, ask trusted colleagues, friends, and family members for feedback. To grow in self-recognition and self-regulation, consider these practices:

- Reflect on whether you tend to "live in your head" and avoid acknowledging the heart because it makes you uncomfortable.

- Before an event, try to label how you feel about it and take a moment to recognize specific thoughts you have associated with that event.

- Pay attention to your body for clues about what you might be feeling: body aches, lethargy, elevated heart rate, and heart palpitations might be an indication of emotional arousal.

- When you feel stressed, identify (and even write out) the thoughts and feelings you have at that exact moment.

Consider your family of origin. How was emotion handled? Did your parents/guardians model that emotions were okay to be experienced, or did they repress and hide emotion? Was there a certain emotion that was not permitted (anger, for example)?

The way we deal with anger—or any emotion, for that matter—as adults is deeply embedded in our family history. If you grew up in a home where experiencing anger was permitted, but it was expressed in a way that was damaging to members of the family (perhaps through physical or verbal aggression, biting sarcasm, shaming, or chronic criticism), then you probably learned to express anger the same way. Or, you may have learned to simply ignore your anger or talk yourself out of it, so now you no longer are able to recognize anger when it knocks. You probably learned to focus on feedback that convinces you that you are doing the right thing by avoiding anger: "You are such a laid-back person. I've never seen you get angry. I love that about you." This tendency only reinforces the limitation.

Unhealthy patterns just like this can develop around any emotion that makes us feel uncomfortable (even happiness). Yes, there can be immediate benefits to stifling emotions. Again, emotions are fuel, and avoiding emotions temporarily relieves us of the psychological work of having to acknowledge and express them, but what long-term

"As we avoid emotion, we lose the authenticity of our human experience. Practically, that loss of authenticity translates into poor relationships between colleagues, family members, and friends."

risks are we running if we do this? As we avoid emotion, we lose the authenticity of our human experience. Practically, that loss of authenticity translates into poor relationships between colleagues, family members, and friends.

Now that you have some general ideas about what it looks like to manage your emotions, let's talk about how to manage your personality.

Managing My Personality

After educators in our workshops take the EASEL, they become much more familiar with not just their ability to experience emotions, but their personality types and the strengths and liabilities associated with them. Not until we've identified the potential weaknesses associated with our personalities can we engage action plans to manage and minimize the limitations associated with them. Let's go back to the five personality types and explore what it might look like to regulate the weaknesses associated with each. This is where the rubber of self-regulation meets the road of life.

Personality Dimension #1: Openness

First, we have Robert, our creative thinker who has no problem thinking outside the box. His weakness is the potential to leave behind those who are trying to follow him, due to his desire to explore and need for change. To limit his potential weaknesses, Robert might consider the following strategies:

- Solicit feedback prior to making decisions; establish accountability around decision-making.

- Next time he wants to change something, wait instead just to see how it shakes out.

- Remind himself of the times he was helped by someone or something that was consistent, predictable, and there for him in his time of need. Instead of thinking of someone who is slow to change as a hindrance, think of them as potentially serving a protective role for a group.

- Key questions for Robert are: 1) Have I actively listened to those who are slow to change? 2) Does the frequency, timing, or degree of this change pose potential harm to the group?

Potential personal biases and triggers for Robert are the fear of stagnation and missing out. For example, the fear of missing out may cause Robert to minimize the input of anyone who expresses a desire to embrace the status quo; he may be inclined to think negatively of them (i.e., *"What a stick in the mud!"*).

Amy, on the other hand, scored low on the Openness to Experience scale. The strengths associated with that include her consistency, predictability, and dependability. Her weakness is potentially missing out on new ideas, strategies, or experiences due to her aversion to change. To limit her potential weaknesses, Amy might consider the following strategies:

- Break her daily routine by driving to work via a new route.

- Try a new restaurant.

- Surprise someone.

- Remember that diversity of thought and experience can add layers of excellence to a process or final product. Newer sometimes is better.

- Key questions for Amy are: 1) Do things need to be freshened up or shaken up in any way? 2) Do we need something different to grow more robustly or vibrantly? 3) How will I know if I've become complacent or stagnant?

Potential personal biases and triggers for Amy are the fear of change and risk. Amy may be inclined to think negatively of people who like change as being flaky or dangerously unpredictable.

Personality Dimension #2: Conscientiousness

Next, Adam is our high scorer on the Conscientious scale, so he is extremely productive and able to get things done. His potential weakness is to relationally disengage because he values completing tasks over connecting with people. To minimize this potential weakness, Adam can practice self-regulation via the following strategies:

- Remind himself of the human factors involved in any tasks he seeks to accomplish.

- Invite others to give their opinion on a project, then consider their thoughts and modify the course or the objective as a result.

- Learning from the strength of the reed: Unlike the mighty oak that is uprooted by the hurricane's winds, the reed's flexibility allows it to remain firmly planted through the storm.

- Realizing that people who may be less task oriented may also be much more capable of maintaining effective relationships throughout a project, particularly when those projects feel like storms.

- Key questions for Adam are: 1) Have I damaged my relationship with anyone in my quest to accomplish this task? 2) Have I expressed gratitude to those working with me on this project?

Potential personal biases and triggers for Adam are fears of not being in control, of failure, of being perceived as inadequate, and of not being perfect. Adam may negatively judge people who score low on this scale as being lazy and lacking a sense of urgency about getting things done.

Unlike Adam, LaTonya scored very low on the Conscientiousness scale. Her strengths include her ability to thrive in a chaotic environment and her capacity to roll with the punches. Her potential weakness are inconsistency, disorganization, and inattention to important details. To minimize these, LaTonya can practice self-regulation by:

- Using a daily checklist to make sure she is getting things done.

- Realizing that people who can get things done can be an asset to an otherwise rudderless ship. Without goals an individual and team will stagnate, and without *achieved* goals an individual or team will grow apathetic and eventually hopeless.

- Key questions for LaTonya are: 1) Have I let people down because I lacked an appropriate sense of urgency about getting things done? 2) Do I need to schedule a task for the same day each week in order to see it get done consistently?

Potential biases and triggers for LaTonya are the fear of being consumed by or losing personal freedom to a project or task. Also, the fear of commitment. LaTonya may unknowingly demonstrate bias against people who like to get things done by dismissing them as "control freaks."

Personality Dimension #3: Extraversion

Moving to the Extraversion scale, we have Angela, who is known as the life of the party and believes that strangers are just friends she hasn't yet met. While she is great at connecting with others, her potential weakness is being too self-absorbed, dominating a discussion, or lacking self-awareness. To minimize these weaknesses, Angela can practice self-regulation with the following strategies:

- Carving out some space for quiet processing time alone.

- When in a group, making a point to practice deliberate listening. When the opportunity avails, ask a question to learn more about another.

- Being aware that the individual who prefers to be alone may have valuable insight about a problem because of their natural propensity to reflect.

- Key questions for Angela are: 1) Have I allowed others in the group to express their perspectives? 2) Am I spending time practicing reflection?

Angela's potential biases and triggers are the fears of being alone and of being rejected or left out. She may be prone to a bias against introverts by perceiving them as insecure and passive.

In contrast to Angela, Thad scored very low on the Extraversion scale and loves to be alone. His strengths include the fact that he comes across as being comfortable and at peace with himself. His potential weakness is being perceived as uncaring, aloof, or unapproachable. To limit these potential weaknesses, Thad can:

- Seek out situations to practice social skills, like visual and verbal interaction over a sustained amount of time. As it becomes more comfortable, he can extend the amount of time spent practicing.

- Realizing that communal living has been woven into how we live our lives, and social skills are necessary for effective group dynamics.

- Key questions for Thad are: 1) Do I need to engage more with those around me? 2) What kind of engagement would be most helpful or is most needed at the moment?

Potential biases and triggers for Thad are the fear of losing time and space and the fear of self-disclosure. Thad may hold a negative bias against extraverts by viewing them as shallow and lacking insight.

Personality Dimension #4: Agreeableness

Next, Kristen scored high on the Agreeableness scale, so she naturally presents herself as kind, accessible, and easy to get along with. Her potential weakness is not setting boundaries and being firm when the situation calls for it. To minimize her potential weakness, Kristen can practice self-regulation by:

- Asserting herself appropriately by setting good boundaries.

- Realizing that boundaries are essential for healthy relationships and that setting boundaries is a respectable practice.

- Learning to tolerate appropriate distance and conflict in relationships when it is needed and helpful.

- Key questions for Kristen are: 1) Should I set a boundary in this situation in order to be healthier—physically, mentally, or emotionally? 2) Am I avoiding someone due to fear of conflict?

Kristen's potential biases and triggers are fears of conflict, rejection, and isolation. Kristen may be prone to harbor bias against individuals who score low on this scale by judging them as uncooperative and ill-willed.

Shelly, though, has no problem setting boundaries. She scored low on the Agreeableness scale, and she is a fierce competitor who can be a great leader. Her potential weaknesses are being abrasive and aggressive, and valuing ideas and winning over relationships. To minimize her potential weaknesses, Shelly can practice self-regulation by:

- Making a point to get to know others, without another objective in mind.

- Realizing that victories are shallow when won at the expense of others, and accomplishments will mean very little if trust is lost in the process.

- Key questions for Shelly are: 1) Am I valuing my desire to win over the need for relational harmony? 2) Will competition or cooperation serve the group more effectively in this situation?

Potential biases and triggers for Shelly include the fear of failure, of loss or losing, and of being taken advantage of. Shelly may demonstrate bias against highly agreeable people by viewing them as weak and vulnerable individuals who are destined to be doormats in life.

Personality Dimension #5: Neuroticism

Finally, Carol is our high scorer on the Neuroticism scale. At her best, we can count on Carol to do her homework, be prepared, and always be on the lookout. We know nothing will ever catch her by surprise. Her potential weakness is that her hyper-vigilance can leave her and those around her on edge. To minimize that potential weakness, Carol can practice self-regulation via the following strategies:

- Starting to distinguish the urgent from the important: Always attend to the important, but think twice about what feels urgent. Remember that not everyone will share the same sense of urgency about a situation, but that doesn't mean they don't care or are not as invested as you.

- Intentionally planning time for both rest and fun into her week.

- Key questions for Carol are: 1) How big of a deal will this really be in an hour? Tomorrow? Next week? Next month? 2) How will I know if I'm overreacting? What is my body telling me about my level of arousal and my need for rest? 3) Am I the only one who perceives this situation as urgent?

Potential biases and triggers for Carol include the fear of being caught off guard and the fear of missing out. Carol may show bias against individuals who score low on this scale by judging them to be uncaring or uninvested.

Rusty, however, scored low on the Neuroticism scale. We know he's cool, calm, and collected. He's generally in control, and we can safely bet that he is never going to die from an ulcer. However, at his worst, he has the potential to come across as flat, detached, and uncaring. To minimize his potential weaknesses, Rusty can:

- Communicate to others that he is, in fact, concerned when problems arise by expressing care and empathy.

- Key questions for Rusty are: 1) Is something more required of me right now? 2) How can I help a situation?

- Potential biases and triggers for Rusty are fear of losing emotional control and of being perceived as impulsive. Rusty may show bias against individuals who score high on this scale by dismissing them as overly emotional and unpredictable.

In my work as a therapist, I have found that the most successful individuals are those who are aware of their personalities and don't seek to change them, but seek to maximize their strengths and minimize their limitations. This is good news for us, right? While we may each like and dislike certain aspects of our personalities, they are not the end of the story. The key to success is found in the management of our individual personalities, and that's something we can all engage in.

Now, let's talk about the third area: managing your stress.

Personality Trait	Low Score: Below 2	High Score: Above 4
Openness The degree to which we are open to new experiences and new ways of doing things	**Preserver** Fear of change; fear of risk	**Progressive** Fear of missing out
Conscientiousness The degree to which we focus on tasks and push toward goals	**Flexible** Fear of being consumed by or losing personal freedom to a task or project; fear of commitment	**Firm** Fear of not being in control; fear of failure; fear of being perceived as lazy or inadequate; fear of not being perfect
Extraversion The degree to which we tolerate sensory stimulation from other people and situations	**Introvert** Fear of losing time and space; fear of self-disclosure	**Extravert** Fear of being alone; fear of being left out or not belonging
Agreeableness The degree to which we focus on relationships and defer to others	**Challenger** Fear of failure; fear of loss or losing; fear of being taken advantage of	**Adapter** Fear of conflict; fear of rejection; fear of isolation
Neuroticism The degree to which we respond to stress and other emotional stimuli	**Resilient** Fear of losing emotional control; fear of being perceived as impulsive	**Reactive** Fear of being caught off guard; fear of missing out

Figure 6: Summary of EASEL Big-5 Personality Traits and Associated Fears

Managing My Stress

Remember, for practical purposes, stress is essentially fear-based. When I am stressed about something, by definition, I fear some form of physical or psychological danger. Take traffic, for example. If traffic is too thick, I'll be late for work. If I'm late for work, I'll get a bad performance evaluation. If I get a bad performance evaluation, I'll get fired. If I get fired, I'll be unemployable, we'll lose our house and everything we have.

Personality Trait	Low Score: Below 2	High Score: Above 4
Openness The degree to which we are open to new experiences and new ways of doing things	**Preserver** Do we need something different to grow more robustly or vibrantly? How will I know if I've become complacent or stagnant?	**Progressive** Have I actively listened to those who are slow to change? Does the frequency, timing, or degree of this change pose potential harm to the group?
Conscientiousness The degree to which we focus on tasks and push toward goals	**Flexible** Have I let people down because I lacked an appropriate sense of urgency about getting things done? Do I need to schedule a task for the same day each week in order to see it get done consistently?	**Firm** Have I damaged my relationship with anyone in my quest to accomplish this task? Have I expressed gratitude to those working with me on this project?
Extraversion The degree to which we tolerate sensory stimulation from other people and situations	**Introvert** Do I need to engage more with those around me? What kind of engagement would be most helpful or is most needed at the moment?	**Extravert** Have I allowed others in the group to express their perspective? Am I spending time practicing reflection?
Agreeableness The degree to which we focus on relationships and defer to others	**Challenger** Am I valuing my desire to win or to be right over the need for relational harmony? Will competition or cooperation serve the group more effectively in this situation?	**Adapter** Should I set a boundary in this situation in order to be healthier—physically, emotionally, or mentally? Am I avoiding someone due to fear of conflict?
Neuroticism The degree to which we respond to stress and other emotional stimuli	**Resilient** Is something more required of me right now? How can I help a situation?	**Reactive** How big of a deal will this really be in an hour? Tomorrow? Next week? Next month? How will I know if I'm overreacting? What is my body telling me about my level of arousal and need for rest?

Figure 7: Summary of EASEL Big-5 Personality Traits and Questions to Explore for Personal Growth

If you trace back something in your life that is very stressful for you, at some level, it will boil down to a fear. For the average classroom teacher, performance evaluations can be very stressful, which is totally understandable. The idea of having an administrator in your classroom, observing your every move, and then giving you a rating that will reflect on your capacities as a professional? Yikes. I recently spoke with a thirty-year teaching veteran in Tennessee. She's an absolute rock star of a teacher who has spearheaded countless efforts to improve instruction and student outcomes in her district, and she is widely recognized as a master teacher and mentor. She told me that her most recent performance review, which was based on a combination of her in-class performance and her students' performance on standardized tests, fell into the lowest-possible category. I asked her if she was devastated. She wasn't, she said, because she knew that over the years she had developed strengths, and she continued to struggle to some degree with certain weaknesses. Her professional identity after thirty years of teaching was both solid and levelheaded. Because her internal psychological landscape had matured over the course of her career as an educator, that same external stimulus—someone evaluating her performance—no longer brought her the significant stress that it might have in the early stages of her career.

While we can take measures to reduce the stress in our lives, the

> "For the average classroom teacher, performance evaluations can be very stressful, which is totally understandable: the idea of having an administrator in your classroom, observing your every move, and then giving you a rating that will reflect on your capacities as a professional? Yikes."

"While we can take measures to reduce the stress in our lives, the fact that we get stressed out will always be a part of what it means to be human. So, the question becomes, how can we make the best use of our stress energy?"

fact that we get stressed out will always be a part of what it means to be human. So, the question becomes, how can we make the best use of our stress energy?

The EASEL Capacity for Adaptive Engaging scale measures someone's innate ability to access stress energy as a fuel source to approach (i.e., "fight") in ways that lead to good outcomes for themselves and others. Individuals who score high have been described as task oriented and able to get things done. Individuals who score low have been described as neglecting responsibilities and passive. To make better use of our stress, we could employ the following strategies:

- **Anticipate.** Think ahead to the people, places, times, and events that will challenge you. Be prepared to respond to them ahead of time so that when the stressors arise, you will not be caught off guard.

- **Get connected.** Consider the source of your stress and ask yourself whether you know anyone who has walked through this before. While the event may be stressful to you, there is a good chance that you know someone who has experienced the issue before, and they may have wise advice for you about how to successfully navigate it. Even if you don't know anyone who can offer you guidance or coaching, there is often tremendous benefit in simply having a listening ear—someone who can empathize with you and offer comfort.

- **Exercise.** As we noted in the Regulation of Self scale, finding some type of physical activity to release our stress energy can be a very healthy outlet. After a good workout or physical activity, we will be more ready to initiate and sustain sleep rather than lying in bed with too much energy and racing thoughts.

- **Set boundaries.** As noted in the action points of the Neuroticism scale, learning to differentiate the urgent from the important is an essential skill if one wishes to set good boundaries. We are managing stress effectively when we set healthy boundaries in relationships, in work, and even in play.

When we access the strategies listed here, we grow our adaptive psychological coping muscles and make the best use of our stress energy. However, stress can also lead us to approach in ways that are hurtful to ourselves and others. For example, attacking, blaming, and criticizing others may relieve some of our stress in the moment, but these behaviors can cause a lot of relational damage. For example, we might think, *"It's his fault I'm in this mess. If he weren't such an idiot, I wouldn't have to be dealing with this right now,"* and then erupt our anger on that person in response. Or we might conclude, *"It's all my fault. I'm such a screw-up."* While taking ownership of our weaknesses is a very healthy practice, exaggeration like this can do damage to our self-perception and cause unwarranted self-hatred.

The EASEL Capacity for Adaptive Disengaging scale measures the individual's innate ability to access stress energy as a fuel source to disengage (i.e., "flight") in ways that lead to favorable outcomes for self and others. Individuals who score high have been described as reflective and considerate. Those who score in the low range have been described as lacking in insight and per-spective. The stress management strategies that are most often associated with adaptive disengaging include the following:

- **Practice self-observation.** These can be difficult ques-tions to face, but ask yourself: What might I be doing to contribute to the problem? How might some of my stress be rooted in an insecurity or fear of mine? What am I learning about myself from being in this stressful situation?

- **Keep perspective.** Practice asking yourself these big-picture questions: How big of a deal will this really be in an hour? Tomorrow? Next week? Next month? How will I know if I'm overreacting? What is my body telling me about my level of arousal and my need for rest? Am I the only one who perceives this situation as urgent?

Thus, there are times when it's appropriate to use our stress energy to disengage (i.e., "flight"), and in doing so, we grow our psychological coping muscles. However, we can also disengage in ways that are hurtful to ourselves and others. When disengaging takes the form of apathy, denial, or refusal to acknowledge our own wrong, we run the risk of harming others and not resolv-ing the problem. Thoughts like *"What do I care? I'm not making a difference anyway. I'm just going to act like nothing is wrong"* are not only mentally and emotionally unhealthy, but also lead to unhealthy relationships.

Becoming aware of your stress management style and how you approach or disengage in stressful situations is a worth-while endeavor for your overall well-being and the health of your relationships. If your default is to approach (i.e., "fight"), which strategy can you practice more of: anticipating, getting connected, exercising, or setting boundaries? If you are someone who is inclined to disengage (i.e., "flight"), can you practice more self-observation or keep the big picture in mind? While we can't remove the reality of stress from our lives, we can absolutely work toward making good use of the energy that stress provides.

Approach ("Fight")	Avoid ("Flight")
• Anticipate	• Self-observation
• Get connected	• Keep perspective
• Redirect the energy (exercise, hobby, etc.)	
• Assert yourself appropriately	

Figure 8: Helpful Stress Management Strategies

Approach ("Fight")	Avoid ("Flight")
• Frequently attacking, blaming, criticizing others	• Frequently denying, rationalizing, or being unable to accept responsibility for wrongdoing
• Frequently splitting or causing dissention among staff	• Cutting off feelings/ apathy

Figure 9: Hurtful Stress Management Strategies

Andrea's Journey Into Self-Regulation

Once Andrea and I helped identify that she was marinating in the emotions of condescension and disgust at work, we needed to help her find a way to keep those emotions from negatively affecting her performance as a teacher. Ideally, we would like to arrive at resolution for those feelings, but in the meantime, we would have to find a way to keep those emotions from ruling her. We started referring to her co-teacher as "Mom" and her principal as "Sister," which was helpful for at least two reasons. First, by underscoring the irony of how deeply our family of origin can influence our interactions as adults, we were able to find some degree of humor in a situation that was full of unpleasant feelings. Second, it reminded Andrea that a good portion of the emotional work she had to do really wasn't about her co-teacher or her principal, but about her actual mother and sister.

Andrea showed up to her third therapy session with a brightness about her. She was eager to jump in.

"Okay, Adam," she said resolutely. "I need results today."

What I heard was *"No pressure, Dr. Saenz, but you better make this worth my time and money."*

"Fair enough," I answered. "Let's see what I've got. We ended our last session by exploring how you can effectively manage the challenging emotion you experience when you're around Mom and Sister at work."

Andrea laughed.

"Are you familiar with a BIP?" I asked.

"As in Behavior Intervention Plan?" she answered.

I nodded yes.

"Yes, I've sat in meetings at school where we've identified students with behavioral needs and then tried to find ways to help them," Andrea explained. "Basically, we try to find different ways for them to deal with their emotions."

"Exactly," I said. "We're going to put you on a BIP."

She laughed again. Laughter was good, especially contrasted with her first fifty minutes in my office just two sessions ago.

"In a nutshell," I continued, "a BIP consists of three simple steps. Step one is to identify a feeling. Step two is to link the feeling with a behavior. Step three is to choose a substitute behavior. We've already done step one—we've identified that the problematic feelings for you at work are feeling condescended to and feeling disgusted. Let's go to step two. What do you do when you feel those feelings around those people at work? Be honest."

She paused. "I guess I don't really do anything. I smile politely, but inside my thoughts go crazy. I'm thinking about what idiots they are, how much I can't stand them, and that I don't really want to be working with them."

"Great. Thank you for your honesty," I told her. "So, it's probably safe to say that your feelings keep you from trusting them, they cause you to assume the worst about them, and since you're masking your feelings with a fake smile, we could also say that they cause you to be inauthentic."

Andrea thought for a moment. "Oh my gosh," she said with her mouth agape. "I'm a such a *bitch*!"

This time I was the one laughing. "No, you're not! Those are fairly typical behavioral responses to those feelings. But let's get to step three, because that's where you'll find freedom. Can you think of anything you can do differently when you feel condescended to or disgusted?"

"I can think of what I *shouldn't* do," she said. "Basically, all of the things I've been doing. Past that, I have no clue. But that's what you're here for, right, Dr. Saenz? Remember, I told you that I need results today."

I laughed again. "Okay, let me see if I can lay out some ideas. One substitute behavior is to observe rather than embrace the feelings. As weird as this may sound, you are not your feelings. Think of them as cars passing on a street. When they've come by in the past, your habit is to hop into them and let them drive your thoughts wherever they see fit. You've identified that your thoughts have been racing toward places that are not very kind. Starting today, when those feelings arise, just observe them and say to yourself, '*Oh. There's disgust. I'm going to choose not to step into the disgust car right now.*'

"So, that's my first recommendation," I continued. "Observe your feelings instead of embracing them. Here's the second thing: When you observe those particular feelings, rather than allowing them to fuel unkind thoughts about others, give thanks for them."

I could tell by Andrea's facial expression that she wasn't buying into this idea.

"I know that sounds weird," I affirmed her skepticism. "But here's the deal. These people are in your life at work and they remind you that you have issues to resolve with your family of origin. That reminder is a gift. Next time you're around them and you feel condescended to or disgusted, observe the feeling without letting it drive your thinking, and say to yourself, *'Ah! There's that feeling of disgust. It's a reminder to me that I still need healing from my relationship with my sister. Thank you for the reminder. I'll make a note to explore this with Adam in our next session.'* What's amazing is that as you find peace and resolution in your relationship with your sister, you'll no longer experience such a strong feeling of disgust for your coworkers."

I could see Andrea's mental wheels spinning, so I continued.

"The first recommendation is to observe and not embrace the feeling so it won't drive your thinking," I summarized. "The second recommendation is to give thanks for the feeling, because it's a reminder to you of areas in your life you will find freedom and peace. Here's the third recommendation: Say something appropriate."

"Wait, what?" she asked, clearly thrown off. "What would I say that could be appropriate?"

"You tell me," I responded. "This is where you learn to shift from rendering fake smiles to offering honest feedback. This is about your integrity."

"Sheesh," she replied. "I have no clue. I was just taught that if you can't say something nice, don't say anything at all."

"I get that," I said, "but there is a time and place to set boundaries. Setting boundaries appropriately is a beautiful act of self-respect. I don't doubt that you are overreacting to your co-teacher and your principal because you have issues with your family, but what if your co-teacher is legitimately condescending and your principal is legitimately unproductively indecisive? If that's the case, they need honest feedback from you, and your fake smile is not doing you or them any favors."

Andrea stared, seemingly unable to fathom the possibility.

"Here's what you might consider," I offered. "Use the 'I-statement' formula: I feel (blank) about (blank) because (blank). For example, you could say to her, '*I feel a little overwhelmed by the recommendations you're making because I feel like I've already got a handle on it. If I need recommendations, though, I'll know who to come to. Thank you.*'"

"What you're saying makes sense," she said. "I just don't know whether I'll be able to do it. It seems so, I don't know, bold. Or maybe even rude."

"It's definitely bold," I replied. "Setting appropriate boundaries does require some degree of boldness. But it's not necessarily rude. Not if you speak with kindness in your heart. Don't worry, though, this isn't anything you need to put into place right away. Start with just observing your feelings. Once you get better at that, you can practice giving thanks for them. Whenever the time is right, I'm sure you'll be able to give good, helpful feedback to set boundaries in a way that is kind to others and authentic to yourself."

She seemed relieved.

"One last thing," I added. "About your EASEL results. I see that you scored high on the Conscientiousness scale. For what it's worth, I score pretty high on that scale too, so let's just take a moment to appreciate that without people like us, things wouldn't get done in this world. The challenge we face, though, is that people who score high on the Agreeableness scale drive us crazy. We're interested in results, but they're interested in relationships. Based on how you've described your principal, my guess is that she would probably score high on the Agreeableness scale. Keep in mind, then, that it's not a question of right, wrong, or value. It's just a question of differences. So, you might also start to ask yourself what you can learn from her. Is it possible that she's developing deeper and more meaningful relationships than you? And is it possible that if she is, those deeper and more meaningful relationships will be a huge resource to her and the school at some point?"

Andrea nodded and smiled. I sensed that she was beginning to understand the work she had to do and the freedom that work would earn her.

"So, did you get results? Did I deliver?" I asked as she stood from her seat and began to walk toward the door.

"You did," she answered. "But I kind of wish you hadn't!"

We concluded our session, and Andrea agreed that she would email me when she was ready to come in again. We were hopeful that just as I had learned to use anger to fuel a change in my nutrition and lifestyle, she would learn to use feeling condescended to and disgusted to fuel resolution with her family of origin, and the conflict that had haunted her for years.

My Journey Into Self-Regulation

I pulled into Dr. Steve's parking lot for my third therapy session a week later. No nausea this time, which surely represented progress of some form or another. That's what I told myself, anyway. I did some quick calculations as I made my way into his building and waiting room: I'd been in therapy for a total of one hundred minutes so far, and I'd managed to talk for a grand total of eight of them. According to my calculations, I'd be in therapy until I was sixty-eight.

As we began our third session, Dr. Steve thanked me. "You have tremendous courage, Adam," he said. "Please know I am deeply honored that you have trusted me. You are in control of this process, and we will proceed at your pace."

Session three was decidedly different. The dam was broken, and it was game on. I was all over the place. Why didn't my parents choose to protect, provide, and guide? Why was I always the "bad kid" at school? What could I have done to protect my friend from the sexual assault? Will I ever not be depressed? Who would ever want to marry a man with my past? Even if someone did want to marry me, what could I possibly know about being a good husband and father? The questions seemed endless.

Dr. Steve began to shift forward in his chair. I always wondered if he did that deliberately as a non-verbal cue to his patients that the session was almost over, or if over the years he had just developed a capacity to sit still for exactly fifty minutes at a time, and his body signals a warning at the forty-six-minute mark. Either way, I sensed that our time was nearing a close.

"It's weird," I said wistfully. "For the whole first session, I couldn't even start talking, and now it seems that I can't stop."

Dr. Steve smiled. "Funny how that works, isn't it?"

"Any ideas why?" I asked.

"Oh, absolutely. You were a classic case of bottled-up emotion," he replied. "My guess is that at some point in your life, you decided that feelings weren't worth talking about. What you did over the course of those first two sessions was essentially wrestling off a tightly sealed lid to it all. Very well done."

His insight resonated deeply.

"As far back as I can remember, whenever I told my mom how I felt, it didn't go well. I was met with some version of 'Well, back in my day . . . barefoot, in the snow, uphill both ways', or 'You should just be grateful for . . .' or 'You better get over it real quick before I *give* you something to be pissed off about.' Even when I was happy, if I said anything about it, I would get 'Well, don't be too happy, because life is just waiting to drop the other shoe.' It's like I was damned no matter what I was feeling, so I learned to shut up and go on with my business. Talking never did any good."

"I'm so sorry to hear that, Adam," Dr. Steve replied. "And it's an interesting word you chose—'damned.' In a way, that's exactly what happened: You were dammed, like a massive levee was holding you back. I just want you to know that in here, you are free to feel anything, and you are free to talk about anything. My goal is not to judge you, but to give you strategies to help you better understand yourself and live your life most effectively."

I felt psychologically raw for weeks after each session. There were days I wondered whether I was actually getting worse than better. There were days I didn't want to go to work, didn't want to go to class, didn't want to be around another human being, and days I felt absolutely miserable regardless of whether or not I took my medication. Being honest with myself, and talking about my thoughts and feelings session after session, was like a series of broken bones being painfully reset. The process was not at all pleasant, but it was essential for my proper healing and growth.

> "I never would have predicted it working this way, but the more I share my story, the safer the world feels to me than it did when I kept everything bottled up."

After many sessions over the course of many months, I remember walking into Dr. Steve's office one day and just sitting. Not sitting and avoiding, and not sitting and talking. Just sitting. After about five minutes of this strange silence, I gave Dr. Steve a quizzical look.

"It's funny," I said. "I don't know what to talk about."

"Is it that you have several things to talk about, and you're not sure which to pick?" Dr. Steve asked.

I paused. "Not really," I finally responded. "I mean, I just don't have anything to talk about. There's nothing on my mind. In fact, I haven't even thought about therapy since I left our last session."

If you've ever ridden a rollercoaster, you'll know there is that moment as the train rolls to a stop in the loading station that tells you the ride is over. It's that split second of zero momentum between the time that the cars actually stop moving and the instant the safety bar releases you from your seat. For that ever-so-brief window, there is only still and quiet as you begin to recover from the adrenaline surge and realize, "I did it! I faced my fear! I rode this thing!"

I sensed in that session that our return to silence, right back where we'd started in session one, was the zero-momentum window in my therapy. The ride was over—at least this part of it—and for much of that last session, Dr. Steve and I simply sat and shared a beautiful, quiet peace. Maybe this is what Adam and Eve felt in the garden when they could still be naked and unashamed with one another, before all hell broke loose. Maybe this was just a brief glimpse of paradise right here on earth, as I imagine it might be in heaven.

In the end, I found truth, and it set me free: my parents' divorce? Not my fault, not my responsibility. My friend's murder? Not my fault, not my responsibility. The sexual assault? Not my fault, not my responsibility. But my future—the rest of my life and what happens to me? No one else's fault, and wholly my responsibility. I learned that I could talk about my feelings with someone safe, and in talking about them, those difficult feelings had less power over me. I've been privileged to have shared my story with educators across the world, and as difficult as it still is to do so, it seems like it gets a little bit easier each time. I never could have predicted it would work this way, but the more I share my story, the safer the world feels to me than it did when I kept everything bottled up. John Steinbeck once noted that you can only understand people if you feel them in yourself, and I agree. Once I was finally able to identify and regulate my own feelings, I was more able to understand people around me. I was on a long journey to becoming a more empathetic person.

Chapter 3: The Down and Dirty

- Once we've learned to identify emotions, we can then learn to manage them. I wasn't successful with healthy eating until I learned to identify and manage the emotions I experienced in response to food.

- It is not possible to consciously identify and manage every emotion we experience. However, when an emotion interferes with me doing what I need to do as a responsible adult, or if an emotion causes me to do what I shouldn't do as a responsible adult, I definitely need to make changes.

- Once we've identified our basic personality type, we can take steps to minimize the limitations and liabilities that are associated with our personalities. We can also identify fears associated with our personalities and take steps to limit how much our fears contribute to our biases.

- Stress is very similar to fear, and it is another emotion that we need to manage. Stress places us in fight-or-flight mode. Since we can fight or flee in ways that are helpful or hurtful, we would be wise to think through how we respond to stress.

- Andrea learned to manage the emotions she experienced at school to improve her performance as a teacher and to better understand her coworkers.

- I sat in silence for much of my last therapy session, but this time, the silence was good. As we all become more skilled in recognizing and regulating our emotions, we can hope to experience more peace and feel more empathy for people around us.

Chapter 3: SEL in Real Time

1. What do you know to be true of your personality so far —from various personality tests or feedback from friends, colleagues, and others whom you trust? If you have not yet taken the EASEL Personality Assessment, take some time to do that now. If you have already taken it, review your results, and discuss them if you are in a group.

2. Remember that successful individuals are aware of their personality, accept who they are, and seek to maximize their strengths and minimize their limitations. Describe a specific strength associated with your personality. What is a specific weakness associated with your personality? Identify one strategy (from the examples listed in this chapter) that you think might help you manage this weakness.

3. Write down one to three things you are stressed out about at the current moment. Stressors vary in intensity, from an everyday reality like traffic to a major conflict with a coworker or family member. Try to determine what fear or fears might be behind your stressors. Then write down two helpful coping responses for each stressor.

CHAPTER 4

How Can We Know Others?

Empathy is seeing with the eyes of another, listening with the ears of another, and feeling with the heart of another.

—Alfred Adler, psychologist

In my clinical practice, I recently saw a nine-year-old child (I will call her Micah) who was referred by her pediatrician for psychological assessment. Micah was struggling at school academically and behaviorally, and both her mother and teachers had concerns about her being able to successfully navigate this watershed third-grade year. The purpose of the referral was to pursue diagnostic clarity: Was Micah experiencing a mood, anxiety, or attention disorder?

A standard comprehensive psychological assessment includes several components—including behavioral observations, a clinical interview, review of records, and standardized tests. Behavioral observations can begin as soon as the child and the parent enter the waiting room. What is the child's general activity level? What is their speech pattern? Do they explore the waiting room, or do they remain seated near their parent? If they become too loud or distracting, does the parent offer verbal redirection? If so, how does the child respond?

As soon as Micah and her mother walked into the waiting room, I could hear her—we all could hear her.

"Give me this book!" Micah shouted to her mother as her mother checked in with the receptionist. She was pointing to children's books just beyond her reach.

Micah's mother did nothing to indicate that she heard the request or had any intention of complying with it. Micah continued to speak in a very loud voice.

"Momma, I said, 'GIVE ME THIS BOOK!'" Micah repeated, to no avail.

Micah's mother slowly sat down, and she seemed completely detached from the daughter sitting right next to her. In the few minutes before Micah was scheduled to come back into my office, she ran back and forth in the waiting room, knocking magazines off a table and rearranging chairs. All the while, Micah's mother did virtually nothing to redirect or contain her.

I felt a sense of annoyance, maybe even indignation, arise within me as I heard the commotion in the waiting room. *This is ridiculous. I'll give you a diagnosis right now: bad parenting. There is no medication to treat that. End of assessment.*

I was growing uneasy with the commotion Micah was creating in the waiting room, so I invited her and her mother back early. Micah and her mother made their way into my office and found their seats. I introduced myself.

"Good morning, ma'am," I offered Micah's mother. "I'm Dr. Saenz. It's very nice to meet you."

"Hello. I'm Margaret." Micah's mother offered a weak smile and extended a limp hand. Her eye contact was poor, her affect was flat, and she seemed totally exhausted.

"Tell me what brings you in today, Margaret," I asked.

Micah's mother immediately broke down in tears.

"I'm so sorry," she said, apologizing for her inability to speak as she reached for the box of tissues I kept on the table.

I immediately realized that something much deeper was going on. "Please, take your time," I reassured her. Micah's mother collected herself.

"Well, it's been a long year. *Two* long years, really. It started when Micah's father was diagnosed with cancer," she told me through deep sighs. "We'd hoped to have more time with him, but it didn't work out that way. It seems like our kids are still in a state of shock. I know I am. Micah seems to be responding differently. Since her dad died, her siblings have been quiet and withdrawn, but Micah has gone in the opposite direction. She ramped up, and it seems like everything I've tried hasn't helped. She was so close to her father. They had a beautiful relationship—they were both the high-energy live wires in the family. I know she's devastated. I'm sorry I'm so emotional. I just met with our attorney and a financial planner. To be honest, it's not looking good."

The interview continued from there, but I was overwhelmed by a sense of shame and embarrassment. I had completely misjudged the situation. My laziness and cynicism led me to draw conclusions about the situation that were both premature and false. Given the season of this woman's life—the loss and the challenges she was facing—how could she be on her A game with regards to parenting?

I wish I could say that was the first time I have misjudged someone, but the truth is far from that. Early in my career as a school psychologist, I walked away from countless long, emotionally draining meetings with parents of children with severe emotional disturbances thinking, *"Of course your child is struggling. I would be, too, if I had you for a parent."* Harsh, judgmental conclusions like these kept me from being able to truly enter into these families' worlds and help. Rather, they held me apart as a smug spectator with all the answers.

About five years into my work as a psychologist, a major life event awakened me to my lack of empathy and my need for it. We adopted our daughter when she was ten years old, knowing she had an extensive history of physical, sexual, and emotional abuse at the hands of her stepfather. Six months after the predicted honeymoon period of the adoption, reality hit, in the form of a call from her school.

The expression on her face when I found her in the principal's office immediately answered all my questions: *Yes, another fight. Yes, she started it. Yes, she could have made better choices about how she expressed her emotions.* I knew there was nothing to discuss, so I turned to the principal and asked about consequences. There would be two days of suspension—next time it would be three days—and if it happened again after that, we would be searching for a third school, just four months into seventh grade.

I fell asleep that night thinking about her. I thought about her again over coffee the next morning. On paper, we were a match made in heaven. Her biological mother is Caucasian and her biological father is Latino. My wife is Caucasian and I'm Latino.

There would be no birth-order interruptions; she is six months younger than our only biological daughter and a year older than the elder of our two biological sons. We were confident we could meet her needs. I am a licensed psychologist with a specialty in pediatrics. My wife is a registered occupational therapist with specialized training in sensory integration dysfunction. Like her, I experienced trauma in childhood and lived my teen years away from my biological parents. My wife and I were sure that we would be able to connect with her.

I felt many things, but mostly anger. We weren't supposed to be here, having these struggles, now well over two years into this.

I knew that something had to give, and in the quiet stillness of that morning's coffee, I realized: It was me. Looking back, I can see that it's one thing to work professionally with children who have special needs, but it's an entirely different process when those special needs are in your family, lying with muddy shoes on your living room sofa, snacking loudly in your kitchen, and cursing you from the backseat of your car. Now *I* was the emotionally exhausted parent sitting in the room with the educators who were serving her. I was the parent sitting in the office with the therapist. Over time, a light bulb finally illuminated for me. I remain deeply grateful to my daughter for many reasons, a primary one being that parenting her taught me to have empathy for other parents of children with special needs.

The Need for Empathy in Your Life

Do you ever make an assumption or judgment about others, without having all the data? Is it possible that you have not entered their story deeply enough to appreciate their struggle? Empathy connects us to others in a way that positions us to be the most effective helpers possible. Empathy lets others know they are seen, heard, and understood, and that in itself can be a powerful intervention. Some would go so far as to argue that empathy alone is the only intervention we can truly offer anyone. In other words, empathy is a way that just about anyone can be of help to someone else who's struggling. Individuals who lack empathy have been identified as frequently exhibiting the following behaviors:

- They find themselves in prolonged arguments.
- They form opinions early and defend themselves vigorously.
- They think that other people are overly sensitive.
- They refuse to listen to other points of view.
- They blame others for their mistakes.
- They do not listen when they are spoken to.
- They hold grudges and have difficulty forgiving.
- They do not work well on teams.

One of the many student safety measures in place at Texas A&M University is the Corps of Cadets escort service. Between the hours of 5 p.m. and 7 a.m., any student can call the Guard Room and request a free Corps escort. Two cadets will meet the person requesting the escort and walk them to most on-campus locations. To be qualified for the service, each cadet must know the answer to the following questions: Where is my fellow student in relation to me? How do I get to that location from the Guard Room? How do I get from that location to the student's desired destination? How do I get from the desired destination back to the Guard Room? Since the cadets live on campus, the answers are intuitive for them. Someone like me, though, who is not quite as familiar with the campus layout and building names, probably would not be nearly as helpful as a cadet. What if I'm not sure where I am on campus, exactly, and I have no idea where you are or where you need to go? What if I have a general idea of where you are, but I'm afraid to go there?

For empathy to happen, we need to have a pretty good handle on our own personal map of emotion: We have to be willing to go there ourselves, emotionally. We'll talk more about this later, but we must realize that we all experience a wide range of emotions, which are neither good nor bad, but are simply part of the human experience. Second, we need to be able to identify and name specific emotions. Identifying our own emotions, *"I know that I am bitter because I can't stop recalling what happened, and every time I think about it, I grow a little angrier at her,"* is the prerequisite for identifying emotion in others: *"Knowing what bitterness looks like and feels like, I can tell that my friend is bitter. Instead of judging or condemning them, I can recall a time when I was bitter and feel with them."*

Think of empathy as knowing the map of emotion: *"I know that I am in [insert emotion] because it looks like [insert description] and it feels like [insert description]."* Knowing the full range of the map of emotion is essential, just like the Corps of Cadets knowing the ins and outs of Texas A&M, because if there are parts of the map that I'm not aware of or that I avoid, I will be no help to someone who is struggling and needs an emotional escort to the location on the map labeled "peace." Empathy means that wherever I am on my emotional map, I can find you on your emotional map and meet you there.

> "Empathy connects us to others in a way that positions us to be the most effective helpers possible."

In my clinical practice, I often notice clients confuse empathy (to feel emotions *with* you) and sympathy (to feel sorrow *for* you). The modern term "empathy" traces back to Greek roots: *en* (in) and *pathos* (suffer). When I empathize with someone, I am quite literally with them in their suffering—or any of their emotions, for that matter. To help distinguish whether we are being sympathetic or empathetic, we can ask ourselves: Am I experiencing a fraction of the same emotion as my friend because I care deeply for them, or am I feeling something totally different?

Awareness of Others' Emotions

Empathy is a key component of emotional intelligence, and as we noted earlier, since empathy can be increased, emotional intelligence can increase. Therapists are taught early on to track language in conversation for indicators of what the client is feeling. Since paying attention to language is a core empathy skill, let's review common facets of language that can clue us in to what others are feeling.

Listening Skills

Listening is not the same as hearing—it's much more. Hearing is what our ears do, but listening is what happens in our minds and hearts with the words we hear. As a general rule, people are naturally good listeners when they are curious and interested in the person with whom they are talking. As you read about the listening skills listed below, think back to someone you've dated that you were really interested in (particularly early on, when you were still trying to impress them). My guess is that the skills named below came rather naturally for you.

Good listeners seek first to understand, not to be understood. As the saying goes, there is a reason we have one mouth and two ears: We should be listening twice as much as we speak. In many situations, an individual listens only to formulate what they will say next, without correctly understanding the speaker's intended message first. In other words, they are not listening to understand, but to be understood, which often leaves the speaker feeling unheard.

Good listeners withhold judgment. If what the other person says causes you alarm, go ahead and feel the concern, but try to avoid thinking (and certainly saying) things like *"Well, that was a stupid move."* Good listening is much more about collecting facts and much less about rendering unsolicited feedback.

Good listeners ask good questions. Yes and no questions can be helpful, but the better questions are usually "why" and "how" questions. In the busyness of our lives, we often default to contingent communication—communication that is contingent on a task or activity (e.g., "Did you turn in your homework?" or "Did you pick up the dry cleaning?"). While that kind of business-management language is necessary for a healthy organization to function effectively, it doesn't deepen intimacy or empathy. Non-contingent communication, however, is more open-ended language, not contingent on an immediate task or activity (e.g., "How was your weekend?" "What do you like most about that musical act?"). Unlike contingent communication, non-contingent communication does deepen intimacy and foster empathy.

Good listeners remove distractions. Put the cell phone away.

Clear your mind of your to-do lists or things to worry about. Maintain good eye contact with your speaker. Let your listener know that every part of your being is present in the moment with them.

Finally, good listeners are not afraid of silence. It's okay if you don't know what to say, how to respond, or if the conversation simply runs out. It's okay to say, "I'm not sure what to say right now, but I am happy just to sit here and be with you." In fact, it may be one of the most meaningful and empathetic things you could say.

Paraverbal communication

Paraverbal communication describes not what we say, but how we say it. Some research suggests that it can hold up to 30 percent of the meaning others take from what we say. The first aspect of paraverbal communication is tone, which can be loaded with emotion. Think back to the last fight you had with your significant other. Did anyone say, "I told you: I. AM. NOT. ANGRY."? In that situation, would you be more likely to believe their words or their tone?

Volume is another aspect of paraverbal communication. Anger, as you might imagine, tends to carry more volume. Sadness generally carries less. Think about how differently you might perceive a student approaching you on a Monday morning and saying loudly, "Ms. Smith, you're never going to believe what happened to me this weekend!," versus the same student approaching you and whispering, "Ms. Smith, you're never going to believe what happened to me this weekend."

The last aspect of paraverbal communication worth noting is the speed of speech. Loud, pressured, racing speech—even at a normal volume—can be an indication of excitement or even mania. In contrast, slow speech can be an indication of frustration or confusion.

Non-verbal communication

Non-verbal communication is everything we communicate without sound. Even when verbal output can be silenced, our silence itself speaks. Non-verbal communication is said to convey up to 50 percent of the meaning others infer in our messages.

Facial expressions are the most universally recognized type of non-verbal communication. In establishing the most basic emotions common to the human experience, researchers have presented facial expressions to groups across cultures, and the following six emotions have emerged as being the most universally recognized: happiness, sadness, fear, anger, disgust, and surprise.

Another key aspect of non-verbal communication is eye contact. Think about the last time you went out to dinner and sat across the table from your spouse or significant other. What message would they have been communicating to you if their eyes had been glued to the football game on a television or repeatedly darting across the room to look at another person? Eye contact is perhaps the primary non-verbal cue that tells another person they have our attention.

A final aspect of non-verbal communication is psychomotor agitation. Is your knee bouncing nonstop through a conversation? Are you shifting in your seat every thirteen seconds? If so, you may be communicating to your listener that you are bored or distracted.

The primary goal in attending to language—listening skills, paraverbal and non-verbal communication—is to gain a better understanding of the speaker's emotional status so that we can then ask ourselves: "When have I felt this way? When have I been in this situation?" The point of these questions is not to offer a verbal comparison (*"So sorry to hear your mother died. I know exactly how you feel. I lost my grandmother last year"*), because that turns attention away from the speaker and back to ourselves. The goal is simply to get some kind of internal landscape or frame of reference in order to increase our understanding of the other person. To develop these empathy skills, practice being curious about others and getting to know their story. Get to know people who are not like you culturally, demographically, religiously, politically, or generationally. Practice asking open-ended questions, such as "How are you feeling today?," "How was your weekend?," or "Is there anything I can do to help you today?"

> "Practice asking open-ended questions, such as 'How are you feeling today?' or 'How was your weekend?' or 'Is there anything I can do to help you today?'"

Awareness of Others' Personalities

If we want to get to know someone more quickly, there is a shortcut: Understand their personality. When we work with district- and campus-level leadership teams, we ask them to complete 360 EASEL profiles, in which each member of the leadership team rates the others. This allows each person to gain an understanding of how they are

> "If we want to get to know someone more quickly, there is a shortcut: Understand their personality."

perceived by those around them and to share their personality profiles with the group.

We know that individuals who score high on the Agreeableness scale are more likely to have higher innate capacities for empathy because they are more likely to desire relational harmony. Fortunately, most teachers score very high on the Agreeableness scale. In contrast, though, individuals who score low on the Extraversion scale may be less likely to develop empathy, since introverts may not expose themselves to enough opportunities where they can practice empathy. Likewise, those who score high on the Conscientiousness scale tend to value tasks above relationships, and therefore may have a harder time developing empathy.

In addition to the broad personality types measured by the EASEL, there are much more direct measures of empathy. The Recognition of Others scale, for example, measures the degree to which someone can accurately identify the thoughts and feelings of others. Individuals who score in the high range on this scale have been described as empathetic, caring, and approachable. Those who score low on this scale have been described as emotionally aloof, detached, and uncaring. The primary liability potentially associated with a low score on this scale is relational isolation. When people that depend on me do not feel seen, heard, or known by

> "Key questions to increase your empathy include the following: Have I gone out of my way to learn more about the people I work with? Have I made it a point to understand the thoughts and feelings or scuffles of those around me, particularly the ones who are most different from me?"

me because I lack the empathy to connect with them, they tend to develop a trust deficit. Individuals who lack empathy have difficulty engaging in nurturing, supportive behaviors toward those around them, leaving those in their world to assume they are on their own. Key questions to increase your empathy include the following: Have I gone out of my way to learn more about the people I work with? Have I made it a point to understand the thoughts, feelings, and struggles of those around me, particularly the ones who are most different from me?

Andrea's Journey Into Awareness of Others

Several months after we created Andrea's BIP, she emailed me. Subject line: "So I Guess I'm Not Fixed Yet." Her last appointment was in November, just before the Thanksgiving holiday. At this point, we were well past spring break and into the throes of standardized testing.

"Well, look at you!" I said with a broad smile as I opened the door to the waiting room. She stood, returned the magazine she was reading to the table, and smiled back.

"I'm baa-ack," she said in a sing-songy voice as we shook hands. My spidey-sense tingled.

We sat down in my office, and without needing any prompting, Andrea jumped right in.

"Well, let me start with the holidays," she began. "After our last session, I was going back and forth about whether I wanted to go home, mostly because I wasn't sure if I was at a place where I could deal with them."

I jumped in. "And by 'deal with them,' you mean that you weren't sure you would be able to experience the emotions they evoke in you without letting those emotions control you in ways that aren't helpful?"

She paused. "I wouldn't have remembered to have phrased it that way, but yes—that."

"Okay, great. Sorry to interrupt," I said. "Go on."

"Well, I decided to go ahead and go," she replied. "I guess I just wanted to jump right in and start practicing this stuff."

I smiled and nodded.

"It was the weirdest thing!" she said. "So, as I'm driving down, the whole way I'm thinking to myself, *'Remember, you have power not to let your emotions hijack you. Remember, when those emotions come up, you are going to set a boundary by excusing yourself to a room to practice your breathing exercises.'* Over and over again, I'm rehearsing this across a four-hour road trip. Well, I get there, and sure enough, like clockwork, as soon as I see my mom in the kitchen she starts in with the questions: 'Why did you drive so late at night? Don't you know it's dangerous?' And there I am, with my college degree and my career and my completely independent adult life, being treated like a twelve-year-old."

Andrea paused, smiled, took a deep breath, and continued.

"But then I *remembered!* I don't have to engage that feeling! I have a choice! So, right away, I went straight to the restroom, and I practiced my breathing exercise. I said to myself, 'I am not ruled by this emotion. I am using this opportunity to express gratitude for the fact that I was able to earn a college degree and enter a career field. I am a functional adult."

A wide grin spread across my face. "Very well done, Andrea. I am so proud of you!"

"So, sure enough," Andrea kept going, "the next day, my sister shows up, and right off the bat, she starts sucking up to my mom and doing her people-pleasing thing. But by now, I was already in the mode of being mindful of my feelings. As soon as I realized I was having thoughts of anger and disgust toward my sister, I did the same thing—excused myself to the restroom, practiced my breathing, and retrained my thinking."

"That's amazing, Andrea," I observed. "How did you feel by the time you drove home?"

"Well, it absolutely wore me out," she confessed. "Having to pay attention to what I was thinking and feeling, and then having to break the cycle, step away, reframe, and then join everything again. I swear, as much time as I spent in the bathroom, my parents must have thought I had stomach problems! But looking back, it was *so* good, really. I mean, I would rather be worn out by doing something that will eventually get easier, than being worn out by my emotions whenever I'm around them. It kind of feels like I'm exercising a muscle I've never used before."

"I love seeing you move in the right direction! You jumped right in and just went for it. Very well done." I paused. "I'm confused, though, because the subject line of your email sounded like you weren't doing well."

"Well, yes, that's something else we need to talk about," she agreed. "Over the last few months, I've really been looking at the teachers around me—especially the first-year teachers. I see them struggling with some of the things I've struggled with in the past, and I keep thinking in the back of my mind, *'You know, I could probably help you with that.'* So, I saw on the district's website that a position has opened for an instructional coach, and I'm thinking about applying for it."

As she ended her last sentence, she took a deep breath and

held it. It was as if she was waiting for me to ask with exasperation, "You're thinking about *what?*"

"That's great, Andrea. Why do you seem so unsure about it?" I asked.

She exhaled. "Well, I'm just worried that this is some kind of reaction to crisis or something. You know? Like what if I'm just thinking about that because I'm trying to bail out of my current role? I just don't know if I'm considering it for the right reasons."

"Well, what I hear in your voice is that you are viewing your coworkers with empathy," I said. "You are aware of them in a way that you probably couldn't have been before you realized some things about yourself. I think that's a great thing! It sounds like you see a version of your former self in your less experienced colleagues, and you want to help. I love it!"

"You know, that's kind of what I was thinking deep down, but I just wasn't sure I could trust it," Andrea reflected. "But when I think about mentoring teachers, I just get so excited. It seems like something I could really be good at."

"I totally agree. This could very well be the next stage in both your professional and personal development."

"So, I'm fixed?" she asked with a laugh.

I smiled. "Not any more or any less than the rest of us. But the advantage you do have over most of the people in the world is that you *know* you have issues to work on, and you're strong enough and courageous enough not just to see those issues, but to hit them head-on and do the work to heal and live your best life."

Andrea is an example of how my life is richer because of my work as a therapist. Her passion and courage inspire me. (She's scheduled for next Wednesday at 8 a.m.)

My Journey Into Awareness of Others

Micah's evaluation ruled out Attention Deficit/Hyperactivity Disorder, Major Depressive Disorder, and Generalized Anxiety Disorder. The behaviors her parent and teacher were seeing were best explained as a very understandable adjustment reaction to the stress associated with her father's death. I recommended that her mother consult with Micah's physician to determine whether a short-term course of anti-depressant medication would be a helpful support to the therapy I scheduled for her with a child therapist in our clinic. As I reviewed Micah's test results with her mother, I couldn't help but wonder how her mother was doing. So, when we concluded the review, I asked.

"Margaret, I can't begin to imagine what the last twenty-four months of your life have been like," I began. "The fact that you are concerned for Micah speaks of your love for her. Forgive me, but I think I would be remiss if I didn't ask: Have you been able to find the care that you need? Do you have anyone to turn to? Remember, one of the most important things you can do to love Micah is to offer her the best version of yourself through this time."

Margaret's eyes immediately filled with tears.

"Honestly, no," she said. "I've been so caught up with taking care of the estate and making sure the kids have been attended to. I don't doubt that I probably need care—professional care—beyond the support my friends and family have offered."

I asked her if she'd like to make an appointment with me.

Three days later, Margaret entered my office for her first session. At first glance, her eyes communicated slightly more peace than I had seen previously. Perhaps it was because she had taken this first important step of her self-care. Most of the first session consisted of her, through a continuous stream of tears, reconstructing the major events of the past two years. Her husband had been her soulmate. Their connection was deep and rich, but she wasn't sure which experience had been more torturous: watching him suffer over those last two years, or living without him now. We seemed to fly through the first session—there was so much to cover—so we scheduled the next session for the following week.

"Welcome back, Margaret," I said as we found our respective seats in my office. She offered a faint smile. "Let me see if I can set up a framework for our time together today. Last week, we discussed what the past two years of your life have been like. To say they were incredibly difficult would be an understatement. You've had to watch someone you love dearly suffer, and now you're having to live without him."

There were no tears, but Margaret remained solemn. "Yes, I guess that's a good summary," she said. She then continued, "I was thinking about our appointment on the drive here. My guess is that over the next however many sessions we have, I will be working through the loss of my husband. And that's great. I know I need to do that. I was thinking that for today, though, I'd really like to talk about the kids. It's so important to me to be present and engaged for them."

"Yes, of course," I responded with assurance. "The time is yours."

She breathed a sigh of relief. "Thank you. I'm just so worried about them. Especially Micah. I mean, I'm glad we ruled out those things with the evaluation—at least now I know there's nothing deeper going on. But I worry. Not just about her, but about the other kids, too. I'm sure they must have felt neglected for the past two years. I'm just so afraid that in neglecting them, I've done even more damage to them. I couldn't bear the thought of—"

She stopped.

"Of them somehow not reaching their full potential because of something you did or didn't do along the way?" I suggested.

She nodded. I paused. It didn't feel like a good time to ask her to talk. So I did.

"I remember when my three kids were still in the diaper, toddler, and preschool stages," I started. "This was before we adopted my daughter, Mya. It was right in that perfect storm of life. We weren't newlyweds, but seven years of marriage hadn't, by any means, made us experts. I was starting my career as a psychologist, working long hours and making enough to pay bills and student loans, but not too much more, and my wife had just started back to work part-time as an occupational therapist. We had three young children—sweet and adorable, yes, but young and needy. It was a lot."

Margaret sat back in her chair, seeming to enjoy being told a story. I sensed that she was also reflecting back to those years in her life.

"So, I have this absolutely crappy day at work," I continued. "I was working as a psychologist for the school district, and I had evaluated a student whose mother was *convinced* that he had Bipolar Disorder and wanted him to qualify for Special Education services. After I did the evaluation, it was clear that the student was perfectly fine at school—it was just his home life that he hated, which drove his problematic behavior. We go back to the meeting to discuss the results, I share my findings, and the mother goes absolutely ballistic. She screams at me that she has her attorney on speed dial, and she threatens to sue me for malpractice and have my license. It was a horrible way to end the workday.

"So, I'm thinking, '*You know what? I'm just going to go home, have a glass of wine, and unwind. Everything will be better."* I laughed. "What do I find when I get home? One of the kids had just tried to flush two rolls of toilet paper down the toilet, and since we couldn't afford to have a plumber come out and fix it, I was on my own. Not what I was hoping for when I walked in the door. By now, I'm taking deep breaths and trying to keep my cool, but I can tell it's like rearranging chairs on the deck of the *Titanic*. I change clothes, find my tools, and I head to the bathroom—mind you, all three kids were right in tow (*'Daddy's home, and he's got his tools. Let's go see!'*). I step into the bathroom, see the watery mess, and reach down to turn off the water valve. As soon as I turn the valve, it breaks and water starts spewing into my face and all over the wall. Much of what happened next was a blur. I may or may not have shouted a profanity that may or may not have included the letters 'M' and 'F,' but I do know that I turned and punched a hole in the wall—right in front of my three children."

Margaret's eyes and mouth were agape. "Are you *serious?*" she asked in disbelief.

"Yes, ma'am," I confessed without reservation. "Sadly, I am serious. Licensed psychologist. Specialization in child development. Leading workshops on behavior management. Dropping F-bombs. Punching holes in walls. As though the plumbing job wasn't enough. Now I have drywall, too."

She sat silently for a few beats. Then, she burst out laughing and asked, "So, how did your kids turn out?"

I laughed with her. "You know what? I guess they're okay! They're all making good grades, and they're all making good friends. Most days, I'd call that a huge victory!"

After the laughter subsided, Margaret paused for a moment of reflection. "So, you have all the education and training to know better, and you hadn't been under nearly the pressure that I had been under, and you still blew it?"

"Oh my gosh. Are you kidding?" I asked. "*Re-pea-ted-ly.*"

"Hmm," she mused, still reflecting.

"I think the reason I share that story with you, Margaret, is just to assure you that as parents, we're not perfect, but we usually default to our best work," I said. "When we fail as parents, it's almost never because we had the ability to have done much better, but chose not to offer our kids the best of ourselves. It's usually because we're trying our very best, but our very best in a given scenario might be limited by any number of factors. I want to explore this more with you in the next handful of sessions, but I'm willing to bet that you have done the absolute best with the hand you've been dealt, and I'm also willing to bet that your children bear no ill will against you for the times you've come up short. Sometimes, our peace lies solely in the fact that we know we've faced our challenges with our best effort."

I could tell by the expression on her face that Margaret was desperately hoping that my words were true. We spent the rest of that session and those that followed getting to the root of her fears about how her children have been impacted by the loss of their father. Looking back, I'm not sure how effective I could have been at entering into Margaret's fear of being inadequate as a parent if I hadn't been able to face my own parenting failures.

Chapter 4: The Down and Dirty

- When I am at my worst and the least helpful with others, it is often because I am lacking empathy for them.

- Empathy allows us to enter into the story of another individual. It allows us to better understand the struggles they've faced and view them with greater kindness and compassion, rather than judgment.

- Listening skills are a key aspect of empathy. We are the best listeners when we are truly interested in and curious about the person we are interacting with.

- Paraverbal communication describes not what we say, but how we say it. Much of what we communicate is not actually in our words, but in our paraverbal communication.

- Non-verbal communication is everything we communication without sound: our posture, our eye contact, and our body movements. Non-verbal communication, like paraverbal communication, usually communicates more than our spoken words.

- Knowing others' personality types can give us empathy for them. Sometimes, when others don't do things the way we would, it is not a question of better or worse, or right or wrong, but indicative of different personality types.

Chapter 4: SEL in Real Time

1. Think back to a character from a movie or television show that elicited an obvious emotional response from you. What was it about the character that made you feel strongly for them? Could you identify with them in any way? Were you fully attentive and interested in learning

about them? (Even if the character is fictional, this is a good example of what having empathy feels like.)

2. Identify a time when someone else entered into your story, listened well, and showed you kindness and compassion.

3. Is there someone who needs your empathy right now?

4. Rate yourself on a scale of 1–10 (10 being the highest) for your listening skills. If you are really brave, ask someone who knows you well to score your listening skills. What paraverbal and non-verbal communication skill can you improve in? Examples include: 1) Making sure your tone and pitch match your words and prove them to be true. If not, choose other words, as your paraverbal communication is often a clue to what you think or feel on a deeper level. 2) Maintaining eye contact with the speaker most or all of the time that they are talking. 3) Limiting body movement when someone else is speaking. 4) Having upright, attentive body posture.

CHAPTER 5

How Can We Engage With Others?

Empathy and social skills are social intelligence,
the interpersonal part of emotional intelligence.
That's why they look alike.

—Daniel Goleman, psychologist

Here's an old one: How many psychologists does it take to change a light bulb? It only takes one, but the light bulb first has to *want* to change. Empathy is about me knowing you. But once I see with your eyes and hear with your ears and feel with your heart, how do I go about regulating—helping—you? As the old joke implies, we really can't control anyone but ourselves, and many would argue that we are only in control

> "Perhaps a more helpful question than 'Can I make you change?' is 'How can I make it easier for you to want to change?'"

of ourselves on good days. So, me trying to regulate you feels pretty far-fetched.

Perhaps a more helpful question than "Can I make you change?" is "How can I make it easier for you to *want* to change?" This is what good therapy is all about: creating conditions that would invite the client to see change as both desirable and attainable. What are those magical conditions? The primary condition is a satisfying relationship. If we, as therapists, can build a relationship with the client in which they feel safe, they are much more likely to engage the personal work of change. This is not to imply that only a skilled therapist is equipped to help someone else—not by any means. It is to say, though, that via appropriate social skills (e.g., how we connect) and conflict resolution skills (e.g., how we re-engage when the connection is ruptured), any individual can create the sense of trust and safety in a relationship that will cause the other to want to maintain the connection—even if that means they must change something about themselves or the way they are acting.

> "The primary condition is a satisfying relationship."

Social Skills Versus Etiquette

A highlight in my many years of training was the summer I spent in residence at Oxford University to complete the requirements for my Doctor of Ministry in Pastoral Counseling. For my doctoral thesis, I developed a psychospiritual protocol to treat anxiety disorders: In essence, how might our understanding of the divine interact with our understanding of ourselves to ease our fears? My residency at Christ Church College provided a dedicated window to finalize my ideas into writing.

The high-table dinner in the Great Hall (*Harry Potter* fans, picture the real-life inspiration for Hogwarts' Dining Hall) is a long-standing tradition at Oxford, in which faculty dine with their students at a table on a raised platform. I would be assigned a seat next to my tutor, Canon Vincent Strudwick, who had recently been awarded the prestigious Lambeth degree by the Archbishop of Canterbury.

In the days leading up to the high-table dinner, I found myself feeling nervous. I wasn't sure what to expect. Having grown up in a low-income home on the Texas-Mexico border, formal dinner meant we would be using wicker holders to keep the potted meat from sagging our paper plates. But a high-table dinner at Oxford? Probably not potted meat and saltines on paper plates. Would they serve tea and crumpets? Would I meet the queen, offer a low, regal bow, and say, while gazing toward the floor, "I am humbled to make your acquaintance, Your Majesty, Ma'am"? What if I messed it up and offered the queen a fist bump instead?

To ease my anxiety, I conducted an internet search: *"How not to make an ass of yourself at an Oxford high-table dinner."* That proved unhelpful, so I refined my search terms: *"Dinner etiquette."* Here's what I found:

- A proper handshake involves eye contact and a three-second firm—not limp or bone-breaking—grip.

- When introducing others, introduce the younger to the older and non-official to official.

- When being seated, never assume, but always ask a woman if you may hold her chair. Sit with your stomach about two hand-widths away from the table.

- Work silverware from the outside inward. If you drop food on the floor, leave it; if you drop a utensil on the floor, pick it up only if it presents a safety risk.

- Hold wine glasses by the stem to prevent body heat from artificially altering the wine's served temperature.

- In European style, utensils don't change hands. Once the food is cut, lower the knife hand toward the plate and raise the food to your mouth with your fork, tines down; cut and eat one piece of meat at a time.

- Do not speak with food in your mouth, and avoid placing more food in your mouth at one time than can be swallowed in three chews.

By the time the high-table dinner arrived, I felt prepared. I had rehearsed my etiquette, ironed my bowtie with the patterned skull and crossbones, and folded my pocket square into a three-tip crown fold. I dressed, nodded to myself in the mirror, and walked out my dorm room toward the Great Hall.

The evening was characterized by more victories than losses. Among the victories: I didn't drop food or silverware, I didn't contribute to the unnatural warming of my wine, and I was caught with food in my mouth only five times (that I counted) during the entire evening. Among the losses: I ended up not fist-bumping the Queen because I ended up not meeting her because she had never been invited. Sadly, neither tea nor crumpets were served.

Figure 10: A selfie of me having tea and crumpets after the high table dinner—I was determined to have them, by God—in my dorm room at Christ Church College overlooking the Meadow Gate.

We need to be clear: The etiquette skills I've just outlined, and only partially mastered, have very little to do with social skills in our present context. Social skills are more about maintaining satisfying relationships, and my guess is that not many of us are deeply connected with anyone primarily because they take small bites and have a three-second handshake. My performance at the high-table dinner likely did very little to solidify or weaken any of my relationships. Social skills are so much deeper than common etiquette. They invite us to think through how we want to engage with and treat each other, and a significant portion of how we treat each other is conveyed by our communication style. Of equal and balancing importance, conflict resolution skills deal with the question: How will we respond to each other when we feel we've been mistreated?

> "Social skills are so much deeper than common etiquette. They invite us to think through how we want to engage with and treat each other, and a significant portion of how we treat each other is conveyed in our communication style."

Social Skill Number One: Knowing Your Communication Style

As we noted in Chapter 4, good empathy is couched in effective listening, and effective listening is couched in my attention to receptive language. Once I've heard you correctly, though, how am I coming across in response to you?

Suppose you are conducting a panel interview for a position that just opened in your department. In an effort to learn more about each candidate's abilities and personality, you ask the infamous question "Why should we hire you?"

The first interviewee responds in a rather quiet voice, "I'm not sure, really." The second blurts out, "You should choose me or you'll be sorry. I deserve a role like this." Then the third, "I know I can't make you hire me, but I hope you'll do the right thing," said with a slight smirk. The fourth: "I believe I would be a good fit for the role, and that I could do the job well without neglecting my other responsibilities."

How would you describe the differences in these statements? What do these answers tell you about the way each individual communicates? Let's classify and explain the communication styles encountered here, in order of their presentation.

The Passive Communication Style

The primary concern of a passive communicator is to not upset anyone. Passive communicators rarely express their own thoughts or feelings, they rarely identify their needs, and they rarely set effective boundaries with others. Since they do not express their feelings, they are prone to repress them, which can lead to numerous psychological and physiological dysfunctions.

Sometimes, passive communicators explode, though, because they've held their tongues for so long. When they do explode, they often feel subsequent shame, guilt, and confusion—which they are too passive to express and end up repressing. Passive communicators tend to maintain poor eye contact, hold a slouched body posture, and speak softly and apologetically. Individuals who score high on the Agreeableness scale may be more at risk for communicating in a passive way.

As undesirable as these traits may seem at face value, most passive communicators maintain this approach for the secondary gain of being perceived by others as easy to get along with and able to go with the flow. What they don't realize, though, is that they can also make others feel exasperated with their inability to communicate directly or effectively. Others may also be prone to lose respect for them due to their inability to express their needs or set boundaries. The passive communicator says things like:

- "Oh, don't worry about it. It was nothing, really."

- "Whatever you want is fine. I don't care either way."

- "You can have it. I didn't want it anymore anyway."

The Aggressive Communication Style

If the passive communication style is about not wanting to upset or offend anyone, the aggressive communication style generally does not care about upsetting or offending. While passive communicators are not normally aware of their needs, and when they are they don't express them, aggressive communicators are hyper-focused on their needs and express them as a priority. This style of communication is about winning at all costs.

Aggressive communication is usually loud, and individuals who communicate aggressively tend to maintain intense eye contact and dominating body language. They also interrupt others frequently, become alienated from others, and have a low frustration tolerance. Aggressive communication is characterized by dominating, threatening, blaming, or attacking. An aggressive communicator often sounds like they are speaking in commands, and when they ask a question, the question tends to sound rude or condescending in tone.

Individuals who score low on the Agreeableness scale are more likely to engage in aggressive communication because they worry very little about offending anyone or being connected to anyone. Also, individuals who score high on the Conscientiousness scale may be at risk for communicating aggressively because they tend to place a high premium on results over relationships.

People who depend on an aggressive communication style focus on what they perceive as favorable results: People tend to do what they demand. However, they are often unwilling or unable to consider the relational damage they do in the process. This communication style makes others feel belittled, defensive, resentful, and mistrusting. This is what it sounds like:

- "You better get this done right now, or it will be all your fault if this project fails!"

- "I'm entitled to this. You owe me!"

- "Don't question or challenge me. I'm right and you're wrong!"

- "I'LL USE ALL CAPS TO SHOUT AT YOU IN WRITING!"

The Passive-Aggressive Communication Style

The passive-aggressive communication style combines the least desirable aspects of the passive and aggressive styles. It begins in deference to the other and turns into subtle or indirect aggression when the individual feels powerless. The passive-aggressive communicator may appear as though he or she wants to cooperate, but they rarely follow it with supportive action. One-on-one communication is characterized by superficial cordiality, but can turn into the silent treatment or spreading rumors. Passive-aggressive communication is marked by facial expressions that don't match the perceived feeling or affect. These individuals are stuck in the purgatory of knowing their needs but being unable to appropriately express them.

People who engage a passive-aggressive communication style focus on the fact that they want to hurt you, but aren't hurting you directly, so they believe they are doing a good thing by exercising control. However, the passive-aggressive communication style leaves others feeling confused, exasperated, angry, and mistrusting. Here are some examples of passive-aggression:

- "We can definitely do it your way." (Then, beneath their breath, "Even though that way is stupid.")

- Said with a smile, "Oh, was it your *favorite* sweater I accidentally ruined in the wash?"

The Assertive Communication Style

The assertive communication style is Goldilocks' just-right balance of passive and aggressive styles. In the assertive mode, the communicator is keen on having their needs met but communicates those needs in a manner that extends dignity and respect to the listener. In the assertive communication style, the speaker indicates ownership of feelings without blaming or condemning the listener. Eye contact in assertive communication is respectfully maintained, with typical volume and pace. Sometimes assertive communication means saying no when saying yes would be the popular, if not necessarily the best, option.

People who communicate assertively feel good about appropriately valuing themselves in order to make their needs known, while rightly valuing their listener so as not to harm them. People on the receiving end of assertive communication may feel disappointed if a boundary is set, but there are positive results as well: They know they can take that person at their word, they know where they stand with that person, and they can respect that person.

The assertive communication style sounds like:

- **Example:** "Please let me consider my options, and I'll get back with you."

- **Example:** "Thank you for reaching out. I'd love to help, but I have a report for work due the next day. I'm sorry, but I can't help."

- **Example:** "I felt sad and hurt when you said the dinner I prepared was horrible because I spent a lot of time preparing it."

  - **Passive response:** "It's okay that you criticize my cooking—I don't do anything well anyway."

  - **Aggressive response:** "If you don't like it, you can eat the leftover dog food. An idiot like you wouldn't recognize tasty food if it slapped you in your ugly face."

o **Passive-aggressive response:** "It's okay if you don't like it. I 'accidentally' dropped yours on the floor anyway."

Four basic communication styles tend to emerge in most analyses of language patterns: passive, aggressive, passive-aggressive, and assertive. Research tells us the assertive pattern is most effective, and the good news is that we can choose which pattern to embrace—remember that emotional intelligence is fluid and capable of being developed. We are wise to note that since the success of the communication is the responsibility of the communicator, mindfully engaging a style that builds the relationship is the goal. Let's walk through the four communication styles, and as we do, think about which one best describes your default way of communicating.

Of these four styles, which one sounds most like you? If you're not sure, ask someone you know and trust to give you honest feedback. If you are consistently coming across as too passive, too aggressive, or too passive-aggressive, it is not likely that you are laying the kind of relational foundation that serves you or others well. Research tells us the assertive pattern is most effective, and since emotional intelligence is fluid and capable of being developed, we can start practicing a new communication style today. Communication styles are critical to the strength and integrity of any connection, particularly when conflict arises.

Social Skill Number Two: Effective Conflict Resolution

After I graduated high school, I found myself with limited work experience, limited education, and relatively limited employment opportunities. The job I finally did land was not what I considered a dream job: a dishwasher in a fast-food restaurant. The closing shift was the worst. I'd walk home at 3 a.m., covered in eight hours' worth of sweat, steam, and grease. Apart from the sheer physicality of the job, I was struck by the psychology of it.

The wait staff was mostly college students, and when they would come into the kitchen to drop off dirty dishes and pick up orders, they would congregate around the corner and gossip—not realizing I could hear everything they were talking about. Three months into the job, I knew who was dating whom, who was cheating on whom, and who was about to quit. It all seemed so petty, so adolescent. Looking back, I think it's safe to say one of the most naïve thoughts I had back then was *"Once I have a college degree, I am going to get a real job in the real world and work with real adults and leave all this teenage drama behind."*

As if.

Fast-forward twenty-five years. I have a Ph.D. in psychology and am sitting in my first faculty meeting. Oh, my goodness—the drama! It didn't take me long to figure out which teacher didn't get voted Homecoming Queen and was still hurt by it, or which teacher didn't get put in the game as quarterback his senior year and never got over it. My disappointment to find grown adults still living in the drama of unresolved conflict was exacerbated when I finally had the ego strength to accept that I was just as guilty as the rest. Apparently, time and college degrees don't fix some things.

The term "conflict" traces back to the Latin roots *con* (together) and *fligere* (to strike), vividly illustrating what happens when we are at odds with one another. We experience conflict with one another for many reasons, but three reasons in particular are relevant to our discussion. First, conflict happens because our personalities differ. When you value completing tasks (high Conscientiousness) but I value free-form abstraction (low Conscientiousness), it is likely that we will experience a striking

> "The term's Latin roots *con* (together) and *fligere* (to strike) vividly illustrate what happens when we are at odds with one another."

together of personalities. When you value time with others (high Extraversion) but I am easily overwhelmed by others (low Extraversion or high Neuroticism), it is likely that we will experience a striking together of personalities. A personality mismatch in any given situation can lead to conflict.

Even when our personalities are the same, we can still experience conflict because our communication styles differ. When one friend implements an aggressive communication style, and the other a passive-aggressive style, there is conflict because one person's words make the other feel attacked and disrespected, but they do not express those emotions appropriately. When you implement an aggressive style of communication and I implement an aggressive style of communication, we will experience a striking together of communication styles, despite our similar approaches.

Finally, even when our personalities are the same and our communication styles are the same, we can experience conflict when we have different goals. Even if we both score high on the Agreeableness scale (meaning we don't like upsetting each other), and even if we both have passive communication styles (meaning we *really* don't like upsetting each other), if we do not share goals on any given task, we eventually will experience a striking together of wills. For what it's worth, two passives engaged in conflict equals high entertainment value.

That striking together of our personalities, our communication styles, and our goals has the potential to wreak havoc—not just on the quality of our connections with one another, but also on us as individuals. Conflict can leave us feeling challenged, defeated, and demeaned, which lowers our morale and may increase relational disengagement and apathy. When an organization has been in unresolved conflict for too long, a climate of mistrust takes root, which hinders teamwork and cooperation.

> "Even though at a core level, most adults understand that conflict can be detrimental, many never develop adaptive conflict resolution skills."

Even though at a core level, most adults understand that conflict can be detrimental, many never develop adaptive conflict resolution skills. There are two common maladaptive responses to conflict that I commonly see in my private practice. I'll use a hypothetical my-mother-in-law-insults-me conflict to illustrate:

1. **Ignore it.** Just pretend that your mother-in-law hasn't insulted your cooking and parenting for the thirtieth time this weekend. Imagine treating a physical wound this way—I just cut my arm for the thirtieth time this weekend, but maybe if I keep ignoring it, whatever is cutting me will magically stop, and the thirty wounds that I have now will magically heal themselves. Not likely. Ignoring toxic culture promotes toxic culture.

2. **Get even.** Don't take that kind of crap from your mother-in-law! Every time she criticizes your cooking or parenting, remind her of what a control freak she is or how many glasses of that cheap chardonnay she slammed before 10

a.m. If you don't want to be that direct, make a passive-aggressive comment under your breath, but make sure she can at least hear the words "It's no wonder your ex-husband—" Fighting toxic culture with toxic behavior promotes toxic culture.

These toxic practices may help us cope in the moment, but they sustain instead of resolve conflict. They erode trust, which creates relational barriers. Ignoring a conflict and exacting revenge do nothing to lay the foundation for a relationship that is life giving and worth retaining.

> "These toxic practices may help us cope in the moment, but they sustain instead of resolve conflict."

What does healthy conflict resolution look like? Fortunately, there are some straightforward steps that resolve conflict effectively. While I will acknowledge that it's not usually easy, it *is* simple.

1. **Make sure everyone is calm.** This is an essential first step. Before any progress can be made, all parties need to be calm. This sometimes means that cool-down time and/or space is the first necessary action. Since the next step requires the two of you to begin processing what happened, if one of you is not calm, it is unlikely that you will agree about what happened, and it is likely that you will escalate, emotionally, in the attempt.

2. **Orient as to what happened.** Once you are both in control of your thoughts and emotions, you can begin to process what, exactly, occurred to create the conflict. The goal here is to determine an objective summary sentence

of what happened. It's important not to get bogged down in the weeds on this step ("No, it wasn't 10:39 when you said I didn't know how to discipline. It was 10:38. I know because I looked at the clock. See? You *never* pay attention to details"). Ask yourselves, "What would a third party say about this conflict?" Try to get a big-picture view with a summary statement like "Words were spoken that were hurtful."

3. **Identify facts, feelings, patterns.** Try to separate what you are thinking and feeling into two different categories, as this practice will help you communicate more clearly. This is a great time to utilize the I-statement. Saying, "You always criticize my cooking and parenting" assigns blame and invites defensiveness. An I-statement allows you to own your emotions and state your concerns in a way that is non-threatening, but authentic: "I feel hurt [feeling] when you make comments about my housekeeping and parenting [fact] because I work very hard to be present for my family [fact]." After you have stated your perspective, remember to listen well enough to be able to repeat back to the person what they said, showing that you both heard and understood. Also, look for patterns. Do you usually get into arguments over the weekends, right after work, or late at night? Patterns can help you assess whether there are other factors involved that need to be addressed. For example, if you find that most conflicts occur late at night, perhaps agreeing to express concerns at a different time might be helpful.

4. **Apologize and forgive.** In most conflicts, there is something that each party contributed and needs to own for

the most effective resolution to occur. It works best if the two would ask themselves, "What did I do or say, or not do or say, that contributed to our fight?" For example, perhaps one party has stuffed, instead of communicated, the frustration they felt from the demeaning comments and become bitter toward the other. Acknowledging and apologizing for our contribution is a powerful and reuniting move. (It's important to note that an appropriate apology is specific, genuinely sorrowful for the harm that was caused, and asks for forgiveness.) Similarly, forgiveness, or surrendering the right we think we have to punish someone, can be difficult but is necessary for the relationship to return to where it once was. Forgiveness is not forgetting or ignoring, but a conscious choice to let go of feelings of anger, frustration, and the desire for revenge. When apology and forgiveness occur, the conflict is effectively dealt with and the error-slate cleaned.

5. **Negotiate.** This step recognizes that both parties are free to feel, think, and believe what they want. But changes may need to be made or boundaries may need to be set around the expression of those feelings to avoid conflict in the future. For example: "It's okay for you not to like how I parent or how I cook. It's not okay for you to make demeaning comments, though. From now on, if you feel that something is lacking, instead of criticizing, I would like it if you offered to help. Or you can feel free to take some time alone and write your concerns in a journal."

6. **Involve a third party, if necessary.** Sometimes we're not able to stay calm when trying to resolve conflict; sometimes we're not able to orient as to what happened, or apologize

and forgive one another. Sometimes we get hung up on one of these steps and can't progress because of an intense emotion, or because it's a complex conflict with many factors. If that's the case, we are wise to invoke the guidance of a third party. Maybe a coworker, a supervisor, a family friend, a religious leader, or a professional counselor. Someone—anyone—whom you both can trust should be agreed upon and brought in, to help bring restoration to the relationship.

You've learned how to identify and regulate yourself. You've learned how to empathize with others, and now you've learned that assessing, and maybe modifying, your communication style returns rich relational rewards by enhancing engagement and connection. You've also learned that when conflict creates relational rupture, conflict resolution skills provide an immediate firstaid. How do we take this knowledge and internalize it, to improve both our personal and professional lives? As teachers, how do we *become* the intervention in the classroom?

Some harbor the misconception that a healthy relationship is characterized by the absence of conflict—not true. In the same way that the definition of physical well-being is not the absence of illness, but the body's capacity to successfully resolve illness to health, the hallmark of a healthy relationship is not the absence of conflict but the relationship's capacity to successfully resolve conflict to peace. Conflict resolution is the roadmap that determines how we will respond to one another when our relationship has been ruptured.

> "The hallmark of a healthy relationship is not the absence of conflict but the relationship's capacity to successfully resolve conflict to peace."

Conflict Resolution Roadmap

1 **Calm Down**

Before you begin, each party needs to be calm. If "cool down" time or space is needed, take it. Effort toward earlier resolution will be unfruitful until both parties are calm and in control of their thoughts and emotions.

2 **Orient as to What Happened**

Try to agree on the big picture of what happened, why there is conflict. Avoid getting lost in the specific details and aim for a one-sentence summary of what happened.

3 **Identify facts, feelings & patterns**

Try to seperate what you are thinking and feeling, and communicate with the I-statement. Also, consider underlying patterns that may be contributing to the conflict.

4 **Apologize & forgive**

Each party asks, "What did I do ro say, or not do or say, that contributed to our conflict?" Appropriate apologies are offered and met with forgiveness.

5 **Negotiate**

Determine the changes that need to be made and/or boundaries that need to be set for future communication.

6 **Involve a third party**

If you can't make progress, invoke the guidance of a trusted and agreed upon co-worker, supervisor, family friend, religious leader, or professional counselor.

Figure 11: Conflict Resolution Roadmap

Chapter 5: The Down and Dirty

- I was once worried that I would make an ass of myself during the high-table dinner at Oxford University. My study of proper etiquette did not yield the social skills I was hoping for so I could better relate to the Queen.

- Social skills are not synonymous with etiquette. Social skills are much deeper skills that allow us to maintain connections with one another. They demand that we think through how we want to treat each other.

- Knowing your communication style is an essential social skill. Do you tend to be passive, aggressive, passive-aggressive, or assertive?

- Mastering conflict resolution is another essential social skill. When we respond to conflict by ignoring it or trying to get even, we make things worse.

- Resolving conflict appropriately actually deepens intimacy and strengthens relationships.

Chapter 5: SEL in Real Time

1. Determine which communication style would best categorize the following statements:

    a. "Don't you DARE look at me that way. I do everything for you!"

    b. "I'm not sure if I will be able to make it today. I will try my best, but can't promise."

c. "Yes, I can do it. I'll do whatever you need."

d. "I really don't care where we eat. It's not like my opinion matters anyway."

2. What is the first word that comes to mind when you think of conflict? Can you identify a real-life conflict involving you or someone you know that was handled appropriately and resulted in continued relationship? Can you identify one that was not handled well? What was the result?

3. On a scale of 1–10, how do you feel about your ability to adequately resolve conflict when the need arises? Is your default reaction to ignore it, or to get even?

4. In the scenario below, walk through how you would advise this husband and wife to resolve their conflict, using some of the conflict resolution steps noted above.

a. Wife: "You always spend more than we have, and I'm sick of it. You're careless and selfish, and I've had enough!"

b. Husband: "If it were up to you, we'd be living at our parents' house just to save money. You never spend on anything and always get mad at me when I do. I'm just trying to have a little fun, for crying out loud."

CHAPTER 6

What Is the EQ-uipped Classroom?

Children have never been good at listening to their elders.
But they have never failed to imitate them.

—James Baldwin, novelist

Something happened to me on Monday, August 25, 2008, that was so significant it literally changed the course of my career. That day was my first day ever as a real, live substitute teacher. Since I am a licensed psychologist, I know the best way to heal from a traumatic event like that is to talk about it. There is so much I could tell you about what an epic failure that day was, but let's start with the lowlights.

I arrived to Ben Milam Elementary in Bryan, Texas, at 7 a.m. that day. I was fired up. I was going to make a difference! I was going to change kids' lives! I could feel it in my bones. Since I had conducted professional development on this campus, and since my kids all attended school there, I knew most of the faculty. I walked in the front door and saw the receptionist, who knew me. I handed her my driver's license so she could make me a visitor name badge.

"Good morning, Dr. Saenz," she greeted me with a cheery smile. "I didn't know you were conducting professional development for us today."

"No, ma'am, I'm not," I responded. "I'm actually here to substitute teach."

She looked surprised. "Really? Well, whose class are you going to be in?"

"Ms. Smith. Third grade," I answered, expecting her to offer me some words of encouragement. Instead, she just stared at me for a second, handed me my driver's license and name tag, rolled her eyes, and said, "Pssh. Good luck with *that*."

I returned my driver's license to my wallet and walked down the hallway. *"Haters gonna hate,"* I thought. But I wasn't going to let this little speed bump ruin my day! No, ma'am. I'm going to make a difference! I'm going to change kids' lives! At 7:45 a.m., the students showed up, and everything I thought I knew went out the window. The students had started back to school the Wednesday before, so this was their first Monday of the school year. What I didn't know was that for whatever reason, the teacher had come in over the weekend to rearrange the students' desks. When the kids walked in, absolute chaos ensued: "Where is my desk? Who is this Latino man with tattoos standing in the front of the class with a desperate look on his face?"

I was ten seconds into my first day, and I was already freaking out. What was I thinking? How had I gotten myself into this? I took a deep breath. *Stay calm. You got this. You're a psychologist with*

Ivy League training. This isn't rocket science—I just needed a behavioral intervention. Everyone knows if you have a room of rowdy, inner-city third-grade students, all you have to do to put the fear of God in them is to write their name on the board.

So, that would be my Tier 1, research-based intervention: I would write kids' names on the board. For those kids who did not have the fear of God put in them when I wrote their name on the board, I would step up to my Tier 2 research-based intervention and play hardball: I would give them a check mark.

Just before lunch, I was trying to make a big, dramatic point to the students about how bad their behavior had been and how disappointed their teacher was going to be with them.

"You know what's really sad," I said to them, my voice dripping in judgmental condescension. "We're going to lunch in ten minutes and let me just count the names on the board—looks like twenty-eight of you will be stuck in here with me at recess."

I paused for dramatic effect. Then a little girl in the back of the class raised her hand. I called on her, expecting that she would be the voice of the classroom's collective repentance.

"Sir," she said in disgust, "there are only twenty-two kids in this class."

The lunch bell rang, and I dismissed my class for lunch. I grabbed my bologna sandwich and extra-large iced coffee and trudged down to the teachers' lounge—a shell of a man by 11:15 a.m. The teacher's lounge was empty when I walked in, so I found the nearest table, and just as I sat down, Ms. Reynosa walked in. Ms. Reynosa had been my kids' kindergarten teacher. I could tell by the look on her face that she didn't expect to see me sitting there, rocking slightly back and forth with "P.T.S.D." written across my forehead.

"Hello, Dr. Saenz," she said, with the sugary sweetness that only a kindergarten teacher can produce. Perhaps overcome with concern at what she saw, she walked over and gently placed her hand on the table. "Is there anything I can do to help?"

I looked into her eyes and felt her compassion. I thought about it for a few seconds.

"Yes, ma'am, there is, actually. I know you don't know me that well," I said with some degree of hesitation, "but I'm going to ask you a question, and I just need you to give me an honest answer."

"Of course," she answered, still oozing kindness.

"Ms. Reynosa, where on this campus do you all keep the red wine?"

She laughed. "Oh, Dr. Saenz, you're so funny!"

"No, really," I responded. "I need a drink. Where is it?"

She wouldn't give it up. Thirty seconds later, another bell rang: time to go back to my classroom. I grabbed my untouched bologna sandwich and extra-large iced coffee and trudged back to my class. Between the teachers' lounge and my classroom, somehow I experienced psychological regression. I hadn't cried in a public school since 1976, but I was about to lose it.

We made it through the afternoon, finally, and the last bell rang. I was beyond done. As the kids shuffled out, sure enough, the last student to get to the door was the one that had been riding me the hardest all day long. His name was on the board immediately, followed by a check mark, a hash tag, an exclamation point, and an inverted star. It basically looked like his name and blotted-out profanity. Just before he got to the door, he turned and looked at me.

"Hey, Dr. Saenz," he said through a smile. "You're pretty cool. You gonna be my teacher again tomorrow?"

I looked him straight in the eye. "Good Lord. I sure hope not."

After the kids were all gone, I collected my things and prepared to leave. The teacher from across the hall poked her head in the doorway. She had been checking on me throughout the day to make sure I still had a pulse.

"Well, Adam. How did it go?" she asked with an enthusiastic smile.

"You know what? I'm going with not so well," I responded. She looked surprised.

"Really?"

"Oh, yes, ma'am," I replied. "Really."

"Okay," she said, trying to rally support. "Let me ask you a couple of questions. How many fights did you have to break up today?"

I thought about it. "Well, none."

"Okay. And how many kids did you have to chase across the railroad tracks behind the playground today?"

I thought about it. "Well, none."

"*Psh!*" she exclaimed, waving me off. "What are you talking about? You had a *great* day!"

Usually, I am on a campus as the expert—observing, interviewing, and collecting the data that will inform intervention recommendations for the tried-everything-and-nothing-worked students. The whole reason I decided to substitute teach in the first place was to get a new perspective, to help me better understand the classroom teaching experience, and to see if my experience would, in any way, change the recommendations I was making. My undergraduate degree is in English, and from there I went straight into the study of psychology. I've never had real experience as a classroom teacher. I wondered if I had become the ivory tower academic who operates purely in theory, with no clue about how a real classroom functions.

I still substitute teach now when my travel schedule allows, but I walked away from that first day in awe of what classroom teachers do on a day-to-day basis. Unless one has actually taught in a classroom, it's virtually impossible to appreciate the personal effort and investment required to teach well. Call it my insecurity about being *that* guy, but I need to convey my respect before I— the not-teacher—launch into a chapter that tells teachers how to teach. Caveats duly noted, let's talk about what SEL actually looks like in the classroom.

What We Need to Know About the Students in Our Classroom

Business experts tell us that modern businesses succeed only if they have the capacity to tolerate the volatility, uncertainty, complexity, and ambiguity (VUCA) of today's marketplace. Psychologists have adapted the term to apply to the context of child development. The young man or young woman—whether age five or nineteen— walking into your classroom today walks in from a world that is far more volatile, uncertain, complex, and ambiguous than even ten years ago, let alone the world I knew as a teenager in the late 1980s. In response, many schools have sought to develop a culture of being trauma-sensitive. Schools are mindfully assuring that all students feel physically, socially, emotionally, and academically safe by addressing student needs holistically—taking into account their relationships, narratives, and starting points.

In addition to a more holistic approach, we're searching, desperately, for a profile that will preemptively identify students most at risk for committing any act of violence. Is mental illness the key factor? Cognitive ability? Race? Socio-economic status? Hours logged on a violent video game? Consider the following statistics compiled by the United States Secret Service regarding school shootings:

- All of the attacks were committed by males

- 98 percent of the attackers experienced or perceived a major loss prior to the attack

- 78 percent of attackers had a history of suicide attempts or suicidal thoughts prior to their attack

- 71 percent of attackers felt persecuted, bullied, threatened, attacked, or injured by others prior to the incident (in several cases, that harassment was described as "long-standing and severe")

- Almost all of the attackers, 95 percent, were current students at the school

- In 73 percent of the incidents, the attackers had a grievance against at least one of their targets

Now, consider these descriptions by adults reflecting on a student days after he took lives by gun violence:

- "We had never seen a problem out of that child."

- "He had helped me carry in Christmas packages last year."

- "At this point, from everything we know, it doesn't appear this kid had the kind of warning signs of someone that you would normally associate with someone involved in something like this."

When we consider the data we've collected, then, including both demographic and descriptive data, the bottom line is that we don't really emerge with a specific profile that we hope would help with early identification and intervention. Perhaps what we can assume from this is that any student is potentially at risk, so our intervention efforts need to be systematically focused. What can we do to help *all* students, without depending on their demographic profile or presenting personality as a potential indicator of need?

Student Self-Awareness

You are already well on your way to becoming the living SEL intervention. You are aware of your emotions—where they come from in your body and the role they play in your life. You understand how to regulate them. You are aware of your personality style and the potential strengths and weaknesses associated with it. You are aware of your vulnerability to stress and how to regulate it. That breadth of awareness alone makes you fully qualified to guide students in their self-awareness. What you're learning about yourself and how to regulate your emotions is SEL algebra, and you'll be teaching SEL math facts.

> "What you're learning about yourself and how to regulate your emotions is SEL algebra; you'll be teaching SEL math facts."

We have several options when we respond to student behavior, including ignoring, inhibiting, invalidating, inviting, and instructing. Inviting emotion facilitates student awareness of emotion (step one of SEL), and instructing emotion facilitates student regulation of emotion (step two of SEL). The ideal option is to use off-task or problematic behavior as our cue to teach emotional awareness.

Ignoring Emotion

Let's explore what it looks like to teach students emotional awareness. Much off-task behavior is driven by emotion—boredom,
anger, fear, or frustration, for example. Remember: Emotion is
energy, and off-task behavior is often a stu-
dent's strategy to release or express that emotion. When a student is chronically off-task
or obviously experiencing emotional turmoil,
an essential question is "What is this student
feeling?" We'll never get there, though, if
we're not in the practice of reflecting on our
own emotions. Instead, we will simply **ignore**
emotion. Consider the following scenario: A
student should be reading an assignment, but
instead is talking, loudly and nonstop, to a peer. This is a common
behavior pattern with this particular student.

> "As with most things in life, ignoring problematic emotions won't make them go away."

> **Teacher:** "I need you to stop talking and get back
> to work, please."

> **Student [in an angry voice]:** "I need you to quit making
> us do these stupid reading assignments!"

> **Teacher:** "Maybe you'd rather read in detention.
> Do you want one? I'll give you one."

> **Student:** "Whatever."

> **Teacher:** "Fine. Consider it done."

Since there is no discussion of the student's feelings here,
we have missed an opportunity; instead of SEL learning, these
scenarios of off-task behavior will be nothing more than power

struggles in which the teacher and student learn to dislike and even resent each other. As with most things in life, ignoring problematic emotions won't make them go away.

Inhibiting Emotion

Sometimes, we don't ignore emotions, but we do **inhibit** them. Inhibiting emotion happens when we acknowledge emotion and then send a clear message that emotions are not welcome. In effect, "I recognize your emotions, but I want you to stuff them or repress them because they don't belong here. I don't want to have to recognize them again." Back to our scenario:

> **Teacher:** "I need you to stop, please."
>
> **Student [in an angry voice]:** "I need you to quit making us do these stupid reading assignments!"
>
> **Teacher:** "I don't know what your problem is, but you need to get over it and get to work."
>
> **Student:** "Whatever."

The teacher vaguely acknowledges emotion by suggesting that the student has a problem, but the teacher's response leaves no room for instruction: By directing the student to "get over it and get to work," the teacher misses the opportunity for SEL instruction. The takeaway for the student is that emotions are not welcome. When we teach students to inhibit their emotion, we are teaching them emotional constipation, and inhibited or repressed emotion tends to be internally destructive (as in mood and/or anxiety disorders) and, when finally expressed, it tends to be explosive.

Invalidating Emotion

Another option regarding emotions is to **invalidate** them. We invalidate emotions when we communicate that students are free to express emotion, but that the emotion is wrong: "You shouldn't feel that way, you should feel this way." Back to our scenario:

> **Teacher:** "I need you to stop, please."
>
> **Student [in an angry voice]:** "I need you to quit making us do these stupid reading assignments!"
>
> **Teacher:** "You shouldn't feel angry. You should feel grateful that you even have the opportunity to come to school and grateful that you have a teacher who cares enough about you to teach you to read."
>
> **Student:** "Whatever."

A basic principle in therapy is that emotions are neither right nor wrong—they simply are. Any individual has the right to feel any feeling in response to any stimulus. Our job is not to judge the appropriateness of the emotion, but to show interest in it, which ultimately positions us to be most effective in our instruction of how to manage it. When we invalidate emotion, we teach students that they cannot trust their emotional landscape. The inferred message the student receives is that since something is wrong with my emotions, something must be wrong with me.

Inviting Emotion

Ignoring, inhibiting, and invalidating emotion keeps students from ever entering into the first phase of SEL: recognizing emotion. To begin SEL instruction in an earnest way, we must **invite** emotion. Inviting emotion tells students, "Your feelings are welcome here." It looks something like this:

> **Teacher:** "I need you to stop, please."
>
> **Student [in an angry voice]:** "I need you to quit making us do these stupid reading assignments!"
>
> **Teacher:** "I'm curious: How do you feel right now?"
>
> **Student:** "I'm feeling angry that I have to do this stupid assignment."
>
> **Teacher:** "Ah, yes. I feel angry too sometimes when I have to do things I don't like. I think I understand why you feel angry."
>
> **Student:** "Well, good, because this sucks."

Make no mistake: Inviting emotion provides no quick fix. In fact, often, inviting emotion can have the Pandora's Box effect of rocking the behavioral boat. This is likely why, in the heat of the moment, it can be so much easier to ignore, inhibit, or invalidate emotion. But the practice of inviting emotion has the subtle but powerful effect of empowering students to know themselves. It communicates that they are entitled to their feelings, and that they are not wrong for wanting to express them.

Inviting student emotion can be incredibly challenging, because of the considerable emotional work necessary on our end as adults. In leading by example, we are tasked with effectively identifying and managing our own emotions as they arise in a potentially escalating situation, and that is no small endeavor.

Students' off-task behavior can lead us through a number of feelings, including anger ("I'm trying my hardest—why can't you appreciate that?"), frustration ("I honestly don't know how much longer I can put up with this resistance from you"), and insecurity ("I'm doing my best work here, and I'm obviously not being successful. Maybe I shouldn't have become an educator").

In our EQ-uipped Classroom workshops, we encourage classroom teachers to post a basic feelings chart, using simple facial expressions—emojis, even—as a guide for students. There is no need to make it complicated; just five or six basic emotions, such as angry, sad, confused, happy, scared, and excited, would be a great start. Instead of ignoring, inhibiting, or invalidating emotion, we can invite emotion by expressing curiosity and asking. When students don't know, we can invite them to identify an emotion on display. If they still can't identify an emotion, we can model empathy with the following script: "Alex, it looks like you're feeling (blank) because (blank)." For example, "Alex, it looks like you're feeling angry because your voice is loud, your fists are clenched, and your eyebrows are furrowed."

Inviting emotion allows us to create a classroom and campus culture in which students know any emotion is safe to experience. It also positions us to enter into the final response to emotion, which is to *instruct* emotion. As students experience emotion, then, we can guide them into the second step of SEL—regulating emotion.

Student Self-Regulation

Let's get back to the idea of a behavior intervention plan (remember Andrea from Chapter 2?), which was presented as a three-step process: 1) Identify a feeling, 2) Link it with a behavior, 3)

Offer a substitute. We're going to expand on that idea a bit here. This is what the process can look like from beginning to end, as we identify the feeling, validate the feeling (an important added step to model empathy), link the feeling with an unhelpful behavior, and then offer a substitute:

> **Teacher:** "I need you to stop, please."
>
> **Student [in an angry voice]:** "I need you to quit making us do these stupid reading assignments!"
>
> **Teacher:** "I'm curious: How do you feel right now?"
>
> **Student:** "I'm feeling angry that I have to do this stupid assignment."
>
> **Teacher:** "Ah, yes. I feel angry too sometimes when I have to do things I don't like. I think I understand why you feel angry.
>
> **Student:** "Well, good, because this sucks."
>
> **Teacher:** "It's okay to feel angry. It's not okay to express your anger by disrupting others. Next time you feel angry, you can [offer choices from a preset list of acceptable options, such as 'practice breathing exercises']."

These are the steps broken down in greater detail:

1. **Identify the feeling.** This is to train our hypothetical student, Alex, how to identify and name the emotion he is feeling.

- We might start by asking, "Alex, how do you feel right now?"

- If Alex does not know or cannot accurately identify his feeling, we can provide feedback: "Alex, you look angry right now. I see that your fists are clenched, you're speaking loudly, and you are breathing heavily."

- We can also refer Alex to a feelings chart and ask him to identify his feeling based on what he sees on the chart.

2. **Validate the feeling.** It is important for Alex to understand that he is entitled to any feelings he may experience, and that he is not alone in feeling that way.

- "It's okay for you to feel angry, Alex. Sometimes I feel angry too when I have to do something I don't want to or don't get what I want."

3. **Link the feeling with an unhelpful behavior.** This helps Alex learn that the problematic behaviors people see are linked to his emotions.

- "When you get angry, Alex, you sometimes threaten to harm others or yourself. Remember, we have talked about how that choice will result in negative consequences for you."

4. **Offer a substitute helpful behavior.**

- "Instead of threatening to hurt someone, you can [name three options, such as practicing breathing techniques, counting backwards from ten, taking a short walk, going to a predetermined calm-down place on campus, talking to a predetermined listener, making calming statements to yourself]."

As students begin to practice identifying and appropriately expressing emotion, we can move them along in the process by validating and encouraging their progress. I have had some teachers tell me that they don't believe in reinforcing behaviors that students should already know: "He's in middle school, for crying out loud. Why should I praise him or reinforce him for something he should already be doing?" Such protests are often associated with reflections on how "back in my day," and so on.

Teacher Self-Awareness and Self-Regulation

Remember when I mentioned to Margaret that the best thing we can offer our kids is the very best version of ourselves? This also stands true for teachers, and the way we get there is by practicing SEL when we are emotionally triggered. The effects of this are twofold: 1) It's how teachers can care for themselves and prioritize their own health, and 2) Teachers practicing SEL is precisely the way that SEL will spread to their students. Let's take two common experiences for teachers and think through them, then develop an intervention plan for how to respond in a way that makes your best self feel proud.

Scenario One: I Feel Disrespected

When a student is repeatedly disrespectful, saying things like "I don't have to listen to you," and rolling their eyes when you speak to them.

1. **Identify the feeling:** Is it anger? Sadness? Feeling discouraged at this last straw to an already terrible day?

2. **Validate the feeling:** Tell yourself, "This anger, or whatever it is, is okay. Disrespect is wrong and hurtful to both me and my student."

3. **Link the feeling with an unhelpful behavior:** "Normally, I would immediately punish the student to the degree that I feel appropriate in the moment—in this case, missing recess, a silent lunch, and a phone call home. Then, the feeling of anger would probably come out in rudeness toward the student for the next few days, and feelings of frustration and resentment toward my job."

4. **Offer a substitute helpful behavior:** "Though this student may need a consequence, I'm going to first deal with me. I can be angry, but I'm not going to get in the Angry Car and let it drive me. I should give myself time to calm down, so I can feel more confident about my next steps, and not further escalate the situation with my anger." In the time that is taken, there may be other questions that come to mind, revealing other factors that could be involved, such as the student's current family situation, or simple things like "Might they be hungry or tired? Might *I* be hungry or tired?" Otherwise, the time alone is important, as it gives the space needed to identify and process the emotion, and then thoughtfully determine next steps.

Scenario Two: I Feel Overwhelmed

A long, trying day with thirty-three students from 8:05 a.m. to 3:25 p.m. Tutoring from 3:25–3:50 p.m. Parent Conference at

4:00 p.m. Phone call home for problematic behavior at 4:30 p.m. Grading papers until 5:30 p.m. Need I continue?

1. **Identify the feeling**: Do you feel unappreciated? At the end of your rope? Do you feel alone, like it's all up to you? What is the strongest emotion you are experiencing?

2. **Validate the feeling**: "My job is hard. The majority of what I do is not noticed or appreciated. There's a lot on my plate. Any emotion I am feeling because of my circumstances is valid."

3. **Link the feeling with an unhelpful behavior**: "I have the right to feel, and I also get to determine what I do with that feeling. Do I let it drive my actions? Right now, I'm tempted to let this feeling overwhelm me and make me consider quitting on the spot."

4. **Offer a substitute helpful behavior**: "Can I use this feeling to drive a helpful action, such as seeking out help for processing the weight of my responsibility, in order to care for myself? Is there another stress-relieving action or activity that I can build in, like time to exercise?"

In a field where high output is required, self-care of this kind is ever more crucial. It's this practice that effectively deals with an emotion instead of ignoring or invalidating it, enables you to make decisions you won't regret, and ultimately determines the difference between a professional who, on most days, feels healthy and satisfied in their work and one who does not.

Student Awareness of Others

As students grow in their abilities to identify and regulate their emotions, they will also grow as empathetic individuals. We've modeled empathy to our students by giving them permission to feel. We can help them grow in this critical third step of SEL development by finding opportunities to invite them to practice taking perspective. Through writing exercises or group discussion, students can be led with the following prompts: How does it feel to be [a member of a different race, different gender, different nationality, different socioeconomic status]? We can also turn to current events: What do you think [insert name of public figure] is feeling about what happened to them this week?

> "Research shows the more we know about someone else, the less likely we are to harm them. When students experience conflict with each other, the practice they have had with empathy provides a strong foundation for them to handle their conflict. Guiding students through the conflict resolution roadmap shows how to maintain respect for the other, and provides an alternative to destructive means, like violence."

Research shows the more we know about someone else, the less likely we are to harm them. When students experience conflict with each other, the practices they have had with empathy provide a strong foundation for them to handle their conflict. Guiding students through the conflict resolution roadmap shows how to maintain respect for the other, and provides an alternative to destructive means, like violence.

Student Regulation of Others

The next SEL skill can be stripped down to the foundation that it stands on—interacting well with others. Thinking back to Chapter 5, we remember that social skills are not simply common etiquette, but the reflection of a much deeper understanding of how we will treat one another. At a classroom level, the social contract is an ideal strategy to teach students the underlying components of social skills.

The idea of a social contract dates back at least to the 18th-century age of enlightenment. Philosopher John Locke endorsed the idea of a social contract as an agreement between leaders and followers that allows us to feel safe. We agree to create rules, and we agree to accept consequences. What differentiates the rules of a social contract versus the rules of an institution is that the rules of a social contract are created by group members, and not imposed by a higher authority. This results in a greater sense of ownership and responsibility. We can think of the Declaration of Independence as the definitive social contract in the United States.

Safety is the primary benefit of this strategy, but cooperative learning is also enhanced. Social contracts, when implemented effectively, allow us to get the best from one another. At the heart of a social contract is relationship building. Self-awareness is about answering the question "Who am I?" Empathy is about answering the question "Who are you?" Social contracting is about answering the question "Who do we want to be together?"

When our teachers create social contracts in the social contracts in the EQ-uipped Classrooms, we have them take their class through a fairly straightforward process. Teachers typically spend a full class creating the contract early in the school year, and they have described it as being one of the most valued investments they've made.

Figure 12: An example of a social contract, taken from Dove Elementary School, Grapevine, Texas.

We start by having the students answer some questions on paper individually, such as "How do you want others to treat you?" and "How do you want to be treated by the teacher?" Then the students get into pairs to see which ideas they share. After that, the students move to groups of five, with the goal being to create a list of five or so rules that capture their desires. Finally, the classroom comes together to identify the five or six rules that best summarize or capture what everyone feels is most important. The resulting rules are written for all to see in statements that everyone understands, placed on the wall, and signed by each student.

Part of the value of the social contract is that the teacher does not have to be the "bad cop" when rules are broken. Since these are rules that students have created, and were not imposed on students by authority figures, the contract itself and the students' collective agreement serve as the enforcers. Another benefit of the social contract is that it provides an excellent format for successful reintegration into the group. Students who violate the contract are not simply met with loss of privileges or consequences, but can be guided through practices that teach empathy and mend relationships. For example, they can be asked to write a reflection paper that guides them through a series of questions outlined by American psychiatrist William Glasser, who is known for his *Choice Theory* in work with schools: 1) What are you wanting? (How does what you want fit in with our agreement?) 2) What are you doing? (How does what you're doing fit in with our agreement?) 3) Will your current behavior get you there? 4) What should you do differently?

If you are a parent, or someone who works with children, you'll notice these practices are transferrable, and could be helpful in your particular non-classroom setting. Heck, if you lead anyone, adults included, in any way, and have become convinced of the importance of SEL, developing a social contract might be a wonderful strategy for you to employ to set or reset the tone for interactions among colleagues.

Chapter 6: The Down and Dirty

- Not much else in life humbles me like substitute teaching.

- Since students who commit acts of violence do not fit into a homogeneous profile, we are wise to implement SEL interventions with *all* students, and not just those we think might be at risk.

- We can respond to students' emotions by ignoring them, inhibiting them, or invalidating them. None of these options position us to empower students with SEL strategies.

- When we invite students' emotions, we lay a foundation to help them begin to identify their emotion. After we've allowed students to identify emotions, we can instruct them on how to manage their emotions.

- Teaching is incredibly hard work. Teachers need to identify and manage their own emotions in order to care for themselves and be able to offer the best version of themselves to others.

- When students experience conflict, effective and non-violent conflict resolution needs to be taught.

- The social contract is an excellent tool to give students ownership and responsibility regarding social skills and relationship building.

Chapter 6: SEL in Real Time

Below you will find age-appropriate ideas to help students learn to identify and express emotion. While the best intervention is every adult living out a socially and emotionally intelligent life, some intentional instruction will pay dividends in your classrooms, and in our broader communities.

- **Preschool:** Use a basic feelings chart displaying four to six emotions, aimed at helping students begin to learn emotional vocabulary. Ask students to first identify the emotions of characters in a picture book read aloud. Once they have had practice and success identifying different characters' emotions, start to ask students to identify their own emotions. Begin by modeling, using the following format: "I feel [blank] today because [blank]." Teachers can then add new emotions to the collection, introducing each with a short talk or lesson on what that emotion is and examples of why someone might feel that way.

- **Lower Elementary:** Using actual LEGO minifigures, or large pictures of them, ask the class to identify the emotion by the expression on the toy's face. Get creative and name the minifigs "Thoughtful Tom," "Angry Allison," and so on. Be sure to emphasize that every emotion is acceptable, and that emotions themselves are not good or bad. Display an anchor chart entitled "How Do I Feel Today?," and you can use the minifigure heads and names as options. Add this concept to whatever morning routine you have—as something you talk about during your morning meeting or in calendar time. Model what it sounds like to identify emotion: "Today I am feeling a bit like Angry Allison because I got frustrated when my car wouldn't start and I was late to work."

- **Upper Elementary:** Begin by collecting emotion words in a word bank on the board. Send pairs of students on an "Emotion Hunt," where they will search through magazines and books to collect examples of one emotion—these can either be assigned or chosen. They can cut images from magazines, draw examples, or write phrases they find in books that show what a particular emotion looks or sounds like. Invite students to share the posters they create with the whole class, or display these around the classroom. Teachers can use these posters to introduce a "focus emotion" of the month. This can be accompanied by read-alouds, movie clips, and so on. (The Pixar movie *Inside Out* is an engaging way to teach students the powerful role that emotions play in our lives.)

- **Middle School:** Use the Upstairs/Downstairs Brain concept from *The Whole-Brain Child* by Daniel J. Seigel and Tina Payne Bryson to introduce the students to some psychology. The upstairs is responsible for thinking, body control, logic, and empathy, and the downstairs part (that contains the amygdala) is responsible for the fight-or-flight response and basic functions like breathing. Both serve a purpose, and need to be connected by a proverbial staircase to function at optimal levels. The goal is that students will learn to associate their first reaction and emotional response with the downstairs brain, and then be encouraged to walk that emotion upstairs. There, they can apply deeper thinking and logic to the situation, and choose a thoughtful action or response. Give groups of students various highly emotional scenarios. Students will work together to identify the downstairs and upstairs thoughts and actions associated with the situation, and then make a recommendation for a thoughtful response or next step.

- **High School:** Use a current or historical figure of interest to spark discussion on the relationship between emotions and actions. Talk about the power that lies in emotions being properly utilized toward appropriate, and sometimes groundbreaking, action or change. Give students the opportunity to choose from writing a script, spoken word, rap, theatrical performance, and so on. about an issue they feel strongly about, from the point of view of that biographical character or themselves. Host an Open Mic Day where these are performed. Some differentiation can include using pre-scripted plays, and giving shyer students the option to make a comic strip or art piece that doesn't hinge on performance.

CHAPTER 7

If It Is to Be, It Is Up to Me

If we could change ourselves, the tendencies in the world would also change. As a man changes his own nature, so does the attitude of the world change towards him. This is the divine mystery supreme. A wonderful thing it is and the source of our happiness. We need not wait to see what others do.

—Mahatma Gandhi, activist and leader of the Indian independence movement

Education didn't change my life. Educators did.

—Adam L. Saenz, Ph.D., D.Min.

I'm cycling through stages of mild grief as my son, Isaiah, prepares to leave home and begin the task of adulting. "Individuating" is the term we use in the field to define the separating from the values and traditions held by the family of origin to establish one's own. As with my two girls who have gone before him, I know that the nature of my relationship with Isaiah will change as he begins his launch into adulthood. I'm so proud of him and who he's becoming. He's been auto-admitted into the Mays Business School at Texas A&M University with plans to study finance and real estate development.

Perhaps as an act of solace, I've found myself reflecting back to the many hours we spent together. Some things we did together were inherently and purely fun for us, like hunting and fishing. Others were more deliberate and intentional, like his track and field training and keeping up with his academics.

We planted a garden once, when he was in first grade. It was a project for The Dream Team, a student organization created by his rock star teacher, Ms. Reynosa. The idea was to plant a small garden in their backyards and raise vegetables to donate to the local food pantry. The idea sounded great when my son initially presented it to me. Then I started thinking about it: I know nothing about gardening. I imagined sweating ourselves almost to death in order to plan a pathetic little garden that would probably, somehow and someway, end up *contributing* to the problem of hunger—if only because of the time we would waste on it.

I didn't reveal my reservations to him, of course, and as any parent who didn't want to be a dream-crusher would, I supported him and we went for it. We decided that we would grow tomatoes, and spent the better part of a Saturday afternoon preparing a five-by-seven-foot plot in the backyard. By Saturday evening, seeds were planted and watered, and our work was done—almost.

While we waited, I prepared our contingency plan: We could surely buy some food to donate when our garden failed to yield anything edible. But much to my surprise, tomato plants found their way around my hopeless vibes and started to grow from the dark soil. *"Look at us,"* I thought, *"single-handedly eradicating hunger in our very own backyard.*" It was glorious. Now that I knew we were actually growing something, I didn't just want to grow any ol' regular tomatoes. I wanted to grow *big* tomatoes. So, I watched videos, read blogs, and talked to my tomato-farmer friend in Pennsylvania.

My non-gardener self turned semi-expert when I realized that the way to help our tomato plants reach their maximum potential was to not actually feed the plant, but to feed the soil. All of gardening (I can just imagine myself speaking from the podium at the Gardeners' Convention) hinges on the soil. If the soil isn't healthy, the plants won't be either.

The tomato plants weren't the only thing taking root, though. The dark side of nature soon did too. And I was not okay with the competition: Nothing was going to take our tomatoes that were well on their way toward solving the problem of world hunger and winning us a Rookie-of-the-Year gardening award.

In the end, we managed to stave off the villains—pesky birds, bugs, and weeds—to grow several baskets of good, healthy tomatoes. I know my son felt good about his contribution, but despite my heroism, I didn't win any gardening awards.

Though I have not yet planted another garden, I have hung on to one thing that is often on my mind as I pursue the work of coaching teachers to become SEL-proficient. It's that we can think of SEL as what makes for the best soil. That is, every student that is planted in a school culture with SEL-rich soil has the maximum potential for growth. In this gardening metaphor, we might think of problematic behavior—aggression, noncompliance, and bullying, for example—as weeds that pop up and have the potential to keep the plants (students) from growing.

Research is telling us that the stick-and-carrot strategy of traditional behavior management is a weed-focused approach, mostly ineffective in the long run. Much like weeds, problematic behaviors, if not taken out at the root, will simply spring back up again. In fact, when those same stick-and-carrot external motivators, like rewards for productivity and employee-of-the-month recognitions, are applied in work settings with adults, they actually have the effect of reducing employee productivity and job satisfaction.

SEL is not just another option in a grab bag. It's something different, and something big. And the way we employ it is also different: It starts with us. We commit to living emotionally intelligent lives, and thereby become healthier ourselves and contribute to the formation of healthier students.

Starting anything new can be a daunting task, but if we can get over that hump, we will soon find ourselves in a rhythm of showing up, committing to check and manage our own emotions, and helping our students do the same. It will start to become a part of who we are, and our students will be greatly impacted by our new habits, with additional boosts of SEL direct instruction along the way.

What I'm talking about is a district full of Life Givers. It's a district where all the Life Suckers have either retired and moved away, or they have secured alternative employment as email spammers who will gladly share their massive inheritance with you if you will only send a small fee to a bank in Nigeria. The Life Giver School District is not life giving because there are no acts of aggression or because there are no acts of noncompliance, or because there is no illogical standardized testing. It is life giving because the adults in the district have committed to living emotionally intelligent lives, thereby making it is a safe place of learning with the richest of soils. This is a place where the last component of SEL, responsible decision-making, comes natu-rally. It's the fruit that springs from the soil.

This last step in our SEL journey is where the picture comes together and makes an impact on the world. We've seen in Colum-bine, Red Lake, Blacksburg, Newtown, Parkland, and Santa Fe—poor decision-making causes irreversible devastation. Responsible and good decision-making by students and educators does far more than prevent violence. It actually has the power to shift an entire culture. Think about it: What would it mean to you if you were able to impact one student, to draw on his understanding of SEL and make a responsible choice when the moment of decision comes?

What might the impact be if a whole group of socially and emotionally intelligent kids grow up to be socially and emotion-ally intelligent *adults*, who work at and lead socially and emotion-ally intelligent companies?

The entire culture of a community has the potential to be changed. What do you think? Are you game for being an agent of this kind of change?

List of Works Consulted

Aal-Barwaliz, M. A., Arbeyat, A., & Hamadneh, B, M. (2015). Emotional intelligence and its relationship with burnout among special education teachers in Jordan: An analytical descriptive study on the southern territory. *Journal of Education and Practice*, 6(34), 88–95

Adalbjarnardottir, S., & Runarsdottir, E. M. (2006). A leader's experiences of intercultural education in an elementary school: Changes and challenges. *Theory into Practice*, 45(2), 177–186

Al-Safran, E., Brown, D., & Wiseman, A. (2014). The effect of principal's leadership style on school environment and outcome. *Research in Higher Education Journal*, 22(1), 1–19

Allen, S. J., Shankman, M. L., & Haber-Curran, P. (2016). Developing emotionally intelligent leadership: The need for deliberate practice and collaboration across disciplines. *New Directions for Higher Education*, 174, 79–91

Anders, S., Lotze, M., Erb, M., Grodd, W., & Birbaumer, N. (2004). Brain activity underlying emotional valence and arousal: A response-related fMRI study. *Human Brain Mapping*, 23(4), 200–209

Aydin, A., Sarier, Y., & Uysal, S. (2013). The effect of school principals' leadership styles on teachers' organizational commitment and job satisfaction. *Educational Sciences: Theory and Practices*, 12(2), 806–811

Bahman, S, & Maffini, H. (2012). *Developing children's emotional intelligence.* Bedford Square, London: Continuum International Publishing Group

Baily, B. (2000). *Conscious discipline.* Oveido, FL: Loving Guidance, Inc.

Barrett, S. B., Bradshaw, C. P., & Lewis-Palmer, T. (2008). Maryland state-wide PBIS initiative: Systems, evaluation, and next steps. *Journal of Positive Behavior Interventions,* 10(2), 105–114

Bartsch, A. (2008). Meta-emotion: How films and music video communicate emotions about emotions. *Projections,* 2(1), 45–49

Bayar, A. (2016). Challenges facing principals in the first year at their schools. *Universal journal of Educational Research,* 4(1), 192–199. doi:10.13189/ujer.2016.040124

Belean, R. D., & Nastasa, L. E. (2017). The relationship between parental style, parental competence, and emotional intelligence. *Transilvania University of Brasov. Series VII, Social Sciences, Law,* 10(2), 181–190

Briesemeister, B. B., Kuchinke, L., & Jacobs, A. M. (2012). Emotional valence: A bipolar continuum or two independent dimensions? *The Authors,* 1–12. doi: 10.1177/2158244012466558

Brinia, V., Zimianti, L., & Panagiotopoulos, K. (2014). The role of the principal's emotional intelligence in primary education leadership. *Educational Management Administration & Leadership,* 42(4), 28–44

Cacioppo, J. T., & Gardner, W. L. (1999). Emotion. *Annual Review of Psychology,* 50, 191–214

Caruso, L. F. (2013). The micropolitics of educational change experienced by novice public middle school principals. *National Association of Secondary School Principals Bulletin,* 97(3), 218–252

Chapman, G., & White, P. (2011). *The five languages of appreciation in the workplace: Empowering organizations by encouraging people.* Chicago: Northfield Publishing

Chapman, G., & White, P. (2014). *Rising above a toxic workplace: Taking care of yourself in an unhealthy environment.* Chicago: Northfield Publishing

Cherniss, C., & Goleman, D. (2001). *The emotionally intelligent workplace: How to select for, measure and improve emotional intelligence in individuals, groups and organizations.* San Francisco: Jossey-Bass

Cheung, F. Y., & Tang, C. S. (2009). The influence of emotional intelligence and affectivity on emotional labor strategies at work. *Journal of Individual differences,* 30(2), 75–86. doi:10.1027/1614-0001.30.2.75

Ciucci, E., Baroncelli, A., Grazzani, I., & Ornaghi, C. C. (2016). Emotional arousal and regulation: Further evidence of the validity of the "How I feel" questionnaire for use with school age children. *Journal of School Health,* 86(3), 195–203

Cliffe, J. (2011). Emotional intelligence: A study of female secondary school headteachers. *Educational Management, Administration & Leadership,* 39(2), 205–218

Corrie, C. (2009). *Becoming emotionally intelligent.* New York: Continuum International Publishing Group

Daga, S. S., Raval, V. V., & Raj, S. P. (2015). Maternal meta-emotion and child socio-emotional functioning in immigrant Indian and White American families. *Asian American Journal of Psychology,* 6(3), 233–241

Daly, L. A., & Perez, L. M. (2009). Exposure to media violence and other correlates of aggressive behavior in preschool children. *Early Childhood Research and Practice,* 11(2), 1–13

Domino, M. (2013). Measuring the impact of an alternative approach to school bulling. *Journal of School Health,* 83(6), 430–437

Domitrovich, C. E., Durlak, J. A., & Weissberg, R. P. (2017). *Handbook of social and emotional learning: Research and practice.* New York: Guilford Press

Dowd, T. E., Clen, S. L., & Arnold, K. D. (2010). The specialty practice of cognitive and behavioral psychology. *Professional Psychology: Research and Practice*, 41(1), 89–95

Duncombe, M. E., Havighurst, S. S., Holland, K. A., & Frankling, E. J. (2012). The contribution of parenting practices and parent emotion factors in children at risk for disruptive behavior disorder. *Child Psychiatry and Human Development*, 43(5), 715–733. doi:10.1007/s10578-012-0290-5

Elias, M. & Arnold, H. (2006). *The educators' guide to emotional intelligence and academic achievement: social emotional learning in the classroom.* Thousand Oaks, California: Corwin

Elias, M., & Zins, J. (1997*). Promoting social and emotional learning: A guide for educators.* Alexandria, VA: Association for Supervision and Curriculum Development

Espelage, D. L., Rose, C. A., & Polanin, J. R. (2016). Social-emotional learning program to promote prosocial and academic skills among middle school students with disabilities. *Remedial and Special Education*, 37(6), 323–332

Faryadi, Q. (2007). *Behaviorism and the construction of knowledge.* Online Submission.

Flippo, T. (2016). *Social and emotional learning in action: Experiential activities to positively impact school climate.* Lanham, MD: The Rowman and Littlefield Publishing Group

Frey, K. S., Nolen, S. B., Edstrom, L. V., & Hirschstein, M. K. (2005). Effects of a school-based social-emotional competence program: Linking children's goals, attributions, and behavior. *Applied Developmental Psychology*, 26, 171–200

Goleman, D., Boyatzis, R., & McKeen, A. (2004). *Primal leadership: Learning to lead with emotional intelligence.* Boston: Harvard Business School Press

Gottman, J. M., Katz, L. F., & Hooven, C. (1996). Parental meta-emotion philosophy and the emotional life of families: Theoretical model and preliminary data. *Journal of Family Psychology*, 10(3), 243–268

Gower, A. L., Shlafer, R. J., Polan, J., McRee, A., McMorris, B. J., Pettingell, S. L. . . . (2014). Brief report: Association between girls' socio-emotional intelligence and violence perpetration. *Journal of Adolescence*, 37, 67–71

Gray, D. (2009). Emotional intelligence and school leadership. *International Journal of Educational Leadership Preparation*, 4(4), 1–3

Gresham, F. (2018). *Effective interventions for social-emotional learning*. New York: Guildford Press.

Gross, J. J., Sheppes, G., & Urry, H. L. (2011). Cognition and emotion lecture at the 2010 SPSP emotion preconference. *Cognition and Emotion*, 25(5), 765–781. doi:10.1080/02699931.2011.555753

Hakim-Larson, J., Parker, A., Lee, C., Goodwin, J., & Voelker, S. (2006). Measuring parental meta-emotion: Psychometric properties of the emotion-related parenting styles self-test. *Early Education and Development*, 17(2), 229–251

Hall, R. C. W., & Friedman, S. H. (2013). Guns, schools, and mental illness: Potential concerns for physicians and mental health professionals. *Mayo Clinic Proceedings*, 88(11), 1272–1283

Hemenway, D., Vriniotis, M., Johnson, R. M., Miller, M., & Azrael, D. (2011). Gun carrying by high school students in Boston, MA: Does overestimation of peer gun carrying matter? *Journal of Adolescence*, 34, 997–1003

Herts, K. L., McLaughlin, K. A., & Hartzenbuenler, M. L. (2012). Emotion dysregulation as a mechanism linking stress exposure to adolescent aggressive behavior. *Journal of Abnormal Child Psychology*, 40(7), 1111–1122

Hitch, C., & Coley, D. (2010). *Executive Skills for Busy School Leaders*. Larchmont, NY: Eye on Education

Hoff, K. E., & Erwin, R. A. (2012). Extending self-management strategies: The use of a classwide approach. *Psychology in Schools*, 50(2). doi: 10.1002/pits.21666

Huang, C., Chiung-Tao, A. S., Hsieh, Y., Feng, J., Wei, H., Hwa, H., & Yenfeng, J. (2017). Cultural perspective on parenting, trait, emotional intelligence, and mental health in Taiwanese children. *International Journal of Emotional Education*, 9(2), 7–16

Hughes, M., & Terrell, J. (2007). *The emotionally intelligent team.* San Francisco: Jossey-Bass

Hurley, R. (2012). *The decision to trust: How leaders create high-trust organizations.* San Francisco: Jossey-Bass

Jager, C., & Banninger-Huber, E. (2015). Looking into meta-emotions. *Synthese*, 192(3), 787–811

Jaleel, S., & Verghis, A. M. (2017). Comparison between emotional intelligence and aggression among student teachers at secondary level. *Universal Journal of Educational Research*, 5(1), 137–140. doi:10.13189/ujer.2017

Josanov-Vrgovic, I., & Pavlovic, N. (2014). Relationship between the school principal leadership style and teachers' job satisfaction in Serbia. *Montenegrin Journal of Economics*, 10(1), 43–57

Jung, H. S., & Yoon, H. H. (2016). Why is employees' emotional intelligence important? *International Journal of Contemporary Hospitality Management*, 28(8), 1649–1675

Katz, L. F., Maliken, A. C., & Stettler, N. M. (2012). Parental meta-emotion philosophy: A review of research and theoretical framework. *Child Development Perspectives*, 6(4), 417–422

Kauts, D. S. (2016). Emotional intelligence and academic stress among college students. *Educational Quest*, 7(3), 149–157

Kearney, W. S., Kelsey, C., & Sinkfield, C. (2014). Emotionally intelligent leadership: An analysis of targeted interventions for aspiring school leaders in Texas. *Planning and Changing*, 45(1), 31–47

Larson, K. E., Bradshaw, C. P., Rosenberg, M. S., & Day-Vines, N. L. (2018). Examining how proactive management and culturally responsive teaching relate to student behavior: Implications for measurement and practice. *School Psychology Review*, 47(2), 153–166

Latif, H., Majoka, M. I., & Khan, M. I. (2017). Emotional intelligence and job performance of high school female teachers. *Pakistan Journal of Psychological Research*, 32(2), 333–351

Le Fevre, D. M., & Robinson, V. M. J. (2014). The interpersonal challenges of instructional leadership: Principals' effectiveness in conversations about performance issues. *Educational Administration Quarterly*, 51(1), 58–95

Lemmens, J. S., Valkenburg, M. P., & Peter, J. (2011). The effects of pathological gaming on aggressive behavior. *Journal of Youth Adolescence*, 40, 38–47

Lencione, P. (2002). *The five dysfunctions of a team*. San Francisco: Jossey-Bass

Lencione, P. (2007). *The truth about employee engagement: A fable about addressing the three root causes of job misery*. San Francisco: Bass

Lencione, P. (2012). *The advantage: Why organizational health trumps everything else in business*. San Francisco: Jossey-Bass

Lenneke, R. A., Alink., Mesman, J., Van Zeijl, J., Stolk, M., Juffer, F., Koot, H., ... Vanljzendoorn, M. H. (2006). The early childhood aggression curve: Development of physical aggression in 10-50-month-old children. *Child Development*, 77(4), 954–966

Leventon, J. S., Camacho, G. L., Ramos Roja, M. D., & Ruedas, A. (2018). Emotional arousal and memory after deep encoding. *Acta Psychologica*, 188, 1–8

Lewis, T. J., & Sugai, G. (1999). Effective behavior support: A systems approach to proactive schoolwide management. *Focus on Exceptional Children*, 31(6), 1–24

Malik, A. I., Zai, C. C., Abu, Z., Nowrouzi, B., & Beitchman, J. H. (2012). The role of oxytocin and oxytocin receptor gene variants in childhood-onset aggression. *Genes, Brain and Behavior*, 11, 545–551

Martini, T. S., Root, C. A., & Jenkins, J. M. (2004). Low and middle-income mothers' regulation of negative emotion: Effects of children's temperament and situational emotional responses. *Social Development*, 13(4), 515–530

McCarley, T. A., Peters, M. L., & Decman, J. M. (2014). Transformational leadership related to school climate: A multilevel analysis. *Educational Management Administration and Leadership*, 14(2), 322–342. doi: 10.1177/1741143214549966

Moore, J. (2011). Behaviorism. *The Psychological Record*, 61, 449-464

O'Brennan, L. M., Waasdrop, T. E., Pas, E. T., & Bradshaw, C. P. (2015). Peer victimization and social-emotional functioning; A longitudinal comparison of students in general and special education. *Remedial and Special Education*, 36(5), 275–285

Ostrov, J. M., Murry-Close, D., Godleski, S. A., & Hart, E. J. (2013). Prospective associations between forms and functions of aggression and social affective processes during early childhood. *Journal of Experimental Child Psychology*, 116(1), 19–36

Parkinson, C., Walker, T. T., Memmi, S., & Wheatley, T. (2017). Emotions are understood from biological motion across remote cultures. *Emotion*, 17(3), 459–477. Retrieved from http://dx.doi.org/10.1037/emo0000194

Pizzo, P. (2018). *Teaching and leading with emotional intelligence*. New York: Teachers College Press

Powell, W., & Powell-Kusama, O. (2010). *Becoming an emotionally intelligent teacher*. New York: Corwin Press

Prati, L. M., Ceasar, D., Ferris, G. R., Ammeter, A. P., & Buckley, M. R. (2003). Emotional intelligence, leadership effectiveness, and team outcomes. *International Journal of Organizational Analysis*, 11(1), 21–40

Price, J. H., Khubchandani, J., Payton, E., & Thompson, A. (2016). Reducing the risk of firearm violence in high schools: Principals' perceptions and practices. *Journal of Community Health*, 41(2), 234–243 doi:10.1007/s10900-015-0087-0

Qouta, S., Punamaki, R., Miller, T., & El-Sarraj, E. (2008). Does war beget child aggression? Military violence, gender, age, and aggressive behavior in two Palestinian samples. *Aggressive Behavior*, (34)3, 231–244, doi:10.1002/ab.20236

Reames, E. H., Kochan, F. K., & Zhu, L. (2014). Factors influencing principals' retirement decisions: A southern U.S. perspective. *Educational Management Administration and Leadership*, 42(1), 40–60. doi: 10.1177/1741143213499254

Richo, D. (1991). *How to be an adult*. Mahwah, NJ: Paulist Press

Ross, D. J., & Cozzens, J. A. (2016). The principalship: Essential core competencies for instructional leadership and its impact on school climate. *Journal of Education and Training Studies*, 4(9), 162–176. doi:10.11114/jets. v4i9.1562

Sanchez-Nunez, M. T., Fernandez-Berrocal, P., & Latorre, M. J. (2012). Assessment of emotional intelligence in the family: Influences between parents and children on their own perception and that of others. *The Family Journal*, 21(1), 65–73

Sayeed, O., & Shanker, M. (2009). Emotionally intelligent managers and transformational leadership styles. *Indian Journal of Industrial Relations*, 44(4), 593–610

Scheff, T. (2015). What are emotions? A physical theory. *Review of General Psychology*, 19(4), 458–464. http://dx.doi.org/10.1037/gpr0000058

Schick, A., & Cierpka, M. (2016). Risk factors and prevention of aggressive behavior in children and adolescents. *Journal of Educational Research Online*, 8(1), 90–109

Shafiq, M., & Rana, A. R. (2016). Relationship of emotional intelligence to organizational commitment of college teachers in Pakistan. *Eurasian Journal of Educational Research*, 62, 1–14. Retrieved from http://dx.doi. org/10.14689/ejer.2016.62.1

Shankman, M., & Allen, S. (2015). *Emotionally intelligent leadership: A guide for students*. San Francisco: Jossey-Bass.

Singh, S. (2015). The impact of emotional intelligence on academic achievement of undergraduate students. *Education Quest*, 6(3), 169–173. doi:10.5958/2230-7311.2016.00003.9

Sinek, S. (2014). *Leaders eat last: Why some teams pull together and others don't.* New York: Penguin Publishers

Somech, A., & Wenderow, M. (2006). The impact of participative and directive leadership on teachers' performance: The intervening effects of job structuring, decision domain and leader-member exchange. *Educational Administration Quarterly,* 42(5), 746–772

Sosnowska, J., Hofmans, J., & DeFruyt, F. (2017). Relating emotional arousal to work vigor: A dynamic systems perspective. *Personality and Individual Differences.* Retrieved from https://doi.org/10.1016/j.paid.2017.06.040

Stewart-Banks, B. Kuofie, M., Hakim, A., & Branch, R. (2015). Education leadership styles impact on work performance and morale of staff. *Journal of Marketing and Management,* 6(2), 87–105

Sugai, G., & Horner, R. R. (2006). A promising approach for expanding and sustaining school-wide positive behavior support. *School Psychology Review,* 35(2), 245–259

Tajasom, A., & Zainal, A. A. (2011). Principals' leadership and school climate: Teachers' perspective from Malaysia. *The International Journal of Leadership in Public Services,* 7(4), 314–333. doi:10.1108/17479881111194198

Thijssen, S., Ringoot, A. P., Wildeboer, A., Bakermans-Kranenburg, M., Elmarroun, H., Hofman, A., . . . White, T. (2015). Brain morphology of childhood aggressive behavior: A multi-informant study in school-age children. *Cognitive, Affective, and Behavioral Neuroscience,* 15(3), 564–577 doi:10.3758/s13415-015-0344-9

Valois, R. F., Zullig, K. J., & Revels, A. A. (2017). Aggressive and violent behavior and emotional self-efficacy: Is there a relationship for adolescents? *Journal of School Health,* 87(4), 269–275. Retrieved from http://doi-org.ezproxy.regent.edu/10.1111/josh.12493

Van Kleef, G. A. (2009). How emotions regulate social life: The emotions as social information (EASI) model. *Current Directions in Psychological Science,* 18(3), 184–188

Warnick, B. R., Kim, S. H., & Robinson, S. (2015). Gun violence and the meaning of American schools. *Educational Theory*, 64(4), 371–386. doi:10.1111/edth.12122

Watts, S. J., Province, K., & Toohy, K. (2018). The kids aren't alright: School attachment, depressive symptoms, and gun carrying at schools. *American Journal of Criminal Justice*, 1–20

Wells, V. K. (2014). Behavioral psychology, marketing and consumer behavior: A literature review and future research agenda. *Journal of Marketing Management*, 30(11-12), 1119–1158. Retrieved from http://dx.doi.org/10.1080/0267257x.2014.929161

Yildizbas, F. (2017). The relationship between teacher candidates' emotional intelligence level, leadership styles and their academic success. *Eurasian Journal of Educational* Research, 67, 215–231. doi:http://dx.doi.org/10.14689/ejer.2017.67.13

Zins, J., Weissbert, R., Wang, M., & Walberg, H. (2004). *Building academic success on social and emotional learning: What does the research say?* New York: Teachers College Press

The Educator Assessment of Social and Emotional Learning EASEL™

Sample Report for Jane Q. Teacher

Congratulations, Jane! You have just taken a significant step toward increasing your capacities as an emotionally intelligent leader. We hope you are eager to review your results. Before we get to the data, though, there are a few important things to remember.

First, traits measured by the Personality Domain are not binary, like eye color—one either does or does not have brown eyes. Instead, think of personality qualities as existing on a continuum, which means that low scores on any given scale do not necessarily identify a weakness, but a different and often competing set of personality traits. You might think of it this way: The question isn't whether you are tall, but the degree to which you maximize for success for the height you *do* have. For example, people with less height might not be as competitive in basketball as someone with a great deal of height, but they likely will be much more effective racing a small sports car. The Personality Domain is about identifying our personality traits, recognizing the strengths and weaknesses associated with each, and taking steps to reduce the risks associated with each of the weaknesses.

Second, remember that the point of the assessment is not to change us to become someone we inherently are not. Instead, the point is to grow to become the best possible version of our authentic selves by recognizing our innate personality structure and mindfully engaging our internal and external worlds to maximize the power of our strengths and minimize the power of our weaknesses.

Third, you'll notice a different format on Personality Domain summaries versus the Emotional Intelligence and Stress Domains. That is because emotional intelligence and stress management styles, while influenced by personalities, are mostly skills-based. That means that they are beneficial behaviors that make our lives better, and that they are skills that we can grow. Unlike the personality traits, low scores on these scales do represent an inherent weakness or a skills deficit that we want to grow.

Fourth, if you're doing a 360 profile, don't overthink outlying scores. It may be that other raters don't know us as well, that they were not appropriately attentive and engaged when responding, or that we simply have a different kind of relationship with them than with the other individuals completing reports. The important thing is to look for patterns: What do the data suggest, broadly speaking? What seems to be the general rule of thumb?

As you read through each scale description, refer to your score summary to see whether you scored in the high, average, or low range on each scale. After scale descriptions, you will receive recommendations for growth based on your scores. If you scored in the average range on any given scale, that simply means that those particular personality traits are not present or absent enough to reflect a true strength or weakness—in other words, you are in a good place of balance.

Now, on to your profile.

EASEL™ Table of Contents

Jane Q. Teacher

Score Summary 215

1. Social Desirability Scale 217

2. Personality Domain

     a. Openness to Experience 218

     b. Conscientiousness 220

     c. Extraversion 222

     d. Agreeableness 224

     e. Neuroticism 226

3. Emotional Intelligence Domain

     a. Recognition of Self 229

     b. Regulation of Self 230

     c. Recognition of Others 232

     d. Regulation of Others 233

4. Stress Management Domain

     a. Stress Resilience Total 234

          i.   Optimism

          ii. Tolerance

          iii. Flexibility

     b. Capacity for Adaptive Engaging 235

     c. Capacity for Adaptive Disengaging 236

EASEL™ Score Summary

Jane Q. Teacher

1. **Social Desirability Scale** _____

2. **Personality Domain**

    a. **Openness to Experience**

    b. Conscientiousness _____

    c. Extraversion _____

    d. Agreeableness _____

    e. Neuroticism _____

3. **Emotional Intelligence Domain**

    a. **Recognition of Self** _____

    b. Regulation of Self _____

    c. Recognition of Others _____

    d. Regulation of Others _____

TOTAL SCORE _____

4. **Stress Management Domain**

    a. **Stress Resilience Total** _____

       i. **Optimism** _____

       ii. **Tolerance** _____

       iii. **Flexibility** _____

    b. Capacity for Adaptive Engaging _____

continued

c. Capacity for Adaptive Disengaging   _____

d. Capacity for Adaptive Engaging   _____

e. Capacity for Adaptive Disengaging   _____

EASEL™:
1. Social Desirability Scale

Jane Q. Teacher

1. SOCIAL DESIRABILITY

High Score > 4; Low Score < 2

The Social Desirability scale measures the degree to which you rated yourself favorably or unfavorably. If you scored in the high range, it is possible that you have approached the test to portray yourself in the most favorable light. While it may be true that you are a saint—individuals with strong religious affiliation often score high on this scale—you may need to explore whether you've overestimated your virtue for fear of being judged or deemed inadequate. By contrast, if you scored in the low range, you may have underestimated your personal virtue and think too lowly of yourself. A 360 assessment can be valuable in helping you to gain a more comprehensive view of yourself.

EASEL™:
2. Personality Domain

Jane Q. Teacher

2a. OPENNESS

High Score > 4; Low Score < 2

The Openness to Experience scale measures the degree of intellectual curiosity, creativity, and preference for change an individual demonstrates. Individuals who score high on this scale have been described as adventurous, imaginative, and entrepreneurial. Those who score low on this scale have been described as liking predictability and being slow to change.

Potential Strengths

- **(High Score)** Thinking creatively, outside conventional boundaries; exploring and discovering; creatively allocating resources; adjusting well to change.

- **(Low Score)** Consistency, predictability, and reliability;

invoking trust from others because of dependability; strong loyalty; paying attention to detail.

Potential Weaknesses

- **(High Score)** Losing the benefits of consistency and pattern; introducing change too frequently, suddenly, or drastically at the unnecessary expense of others.

- **(Low Score)** Getting stuck in a rut and missing out on opportunity; losing capacity to motivate or excite others.

Action Points to Limit Weaknesses

- **(High score)** Solicit feedback prior to making decisions; establish accountability around your decision-making. Next time you want to change something, wait instead just to see. Continually remind yourself of the times you were helped by someone or something that was consistent, predictable, and there for you in your time of need. Instead of thinking of someone who is slow to change as a hindrance, think of them as potentially serving a protective role for a group. **Key questions**: Have I actively listened to those who are slow to change? Does the frequency, timing, or degree of this change pose potential harm to the group?

- **(Low score)** Break your daily routine by driving to work via a new route; try a new restaurant. Surprise someone. Remember that diversity of thought and experience can bring greater levels of sophistication and add layers of excellence to a process or final product. Newer sometimes is better. **Key questions**: Do things need to be refreshed or shaken up in any way? Do we need something different to grow more robustly or vibrantly?

Limiting Personal Bias

- **(High Score)** Potential blind spots: fear of stagnation; fear of commitment; fear of missing out.

- **(Low Score)** Potential blind spots: fear of change; fear of risk.

2b. CONSCIENTIOUSNESS

High Score > 4; Low Score < 2

The Conscientiousness scale measures the individual's propensity to display self-discipline and to be known for dutiful achievement. Individuals who score high on this scale have been described as orderly and exacting, often achieving against odds. Individuals who score low on this scale have been described as carefree and fun-loving.

Potential Strengths

- **(High Score)** Focused, organized, and able to see projects through to completion; disciplined and dependable; task oriented.

- **(Low Score)** Flexible, spontaneous, comfortable with disorder; good at multi-tasking.

Potential Weaknesses

- **(High Score)** Valuing the completion of tasks over the quality of relationships; potentially stubborn, overly demanding, or obsessive.

- **(Low Score)** Excessively casual, inconsistent, irresponsible, or disorganized; cannot be trusted with leadership tasks.

Action Points to Limit Weaknesses

- **(High score)** Remind yourself of the human factors involved in any tasks you seek to accomplish. Practice flexibility by being open to changing course mid-stream when necessary. Consider the strength of the reed: Unlike the mighty oak that is uprooted by the hurricane's winds, the reed's flexibility allows it to remain firmly planted through the storm. Remember that people who may be less task oriented may also be much more capable of maintaining effective relationships through a project, particularly when those projects feel like storms. **Key questions**: Have I isolated myself or anyone or damaged any relationship in my quest to accomplish this task? Have I expressed gratitude to those working with me on this project?

- **(Low score)** Utilize checklist to make sure you are getting things done. People who can get things done can be an asset to an otherwise rudderless ship. Without goals, an individual and team will stagnate, and without *achieved* goals, an individual or team will grow apathetic and eventually hopeless. **Key questions**: Have I let people down who were depending on me because I lacked an appropriate sense of urgency about getting things done?

Limiting Personal Bias

- **(High Score)** Potential blind spots: fear of not being in control; fear of failure; fear of being perceived as inadequate; fear of not being perfect.

- **(Low Score)** Potential blind spots: fear of being consumed by or losing personal freedom to a project or task; fear of commitment.

2c. EXTRAVERSION

High Score > 4; Low Score < 2

The Extraversion scale measures presence of personality traits such as positive emotions, assertiveness, sociability, and the tendency to seek and enjoy the company of others. Individuals who score high on this scale have been described as outgoing, friendly, and easy to get along with. Extraverts are energized in groups. Individuals who score low on this scale have been described as reserved, serious, and avoiding leadership roles. Introverts are energized in solitude.

Potential Strengths

- **(High Score)** Thriving in large groups and loud, busy spaces; may emerge as a natural leader in group situations.

- **(Low Score)** High threshold for being alone; potentially reflective and insightful.

Potential Weaknesses

- **(High Score)** Too outspoken, aggressive, or shallow; may lack self-awareness and may be prone to dominate a conversation.

- **(Low Score)** Aloof, withdrawn, and uncaring; may demonstrate poor social skills due to a preference for being alone; may not be ideally suited for leadership positions due to difficulty engaging effectively with others.

Action Points to Limit Weaknesses

- **(High score)** Make friends with the quiet; practice internal and external listening skills. Appreciate that the individual who prefers to be alone may have valuable insight about the nature and dynamics of a problem because of their natural propensity to reflect. **Key questions**: Have I allowed others in the group to express their perspectives? Have I gone out of my way to be welcoming to those who otherwise might not want to be part of a group? Am I spending too much time in an overly stimulating environment while not practicing introspection?

- **(Low score)** Seek out situations to practice social skills, such as appropriate and sustained visual and verbal interaction; go out of your way to appreciate the value of group and communal interaction, such as diversity of thought and the multiplying power of synergy. Remind yourself that communal living has been woven into how we live our lives, and individuals with capacity and skills to engage that reality are necessary to effective group dynamics. **Key questions**: Do I need to engage more? What kind of engagement would be most helpful or is most needed at the moment?

Limiting Personal Bias

- **(High Score)** Potential blind spots: fear of being alone; fear of being rejected or left out.

- **(Low Score)** Potential blind spots: fear of losing time and space; fear of self-disclosure.

2d. AGREEABLENESS

High Score > 4; Low Score < 2

The Agreeableness scale measures the presence of personality traits that include compassion and innate trust of others. Individuals who score high on this scale have been described as eager to please and as valuing cooperation over competition. Individuals who score low on this scale have been described as competitive, challenging, and prone to argument.

Potential Strengths

- **(High Score)** Relating to authority by being tolerant, humble, and accommodating; being emotionally accessible, and having a high capacity to build relationships across interpersonal differences; being a good team player.

- **(Low Score)** Persistent, competitive, and independent; having a questioning skepticism that keeps others honest; capable of setting boundaries with others.

Potential Weaknesses

- **(High Score)** Too highly accommodating at times when boundaries need to be set; people-pleasing; being averse to conflict and difficult conversations.

- **(Low Score)** Being brash, abrasive, and aggressive; valuing ideas and winning over relational peace and well-being; being self-centered and combative.

Action Points to Limit Weaknesses

- **(High score)** Assert yourself appropriately by setting good boundaries. Accept that people respect individuals who establish and maintain good boundaries, and boundaries are an essential component to any healthy relationship. Learn to tolerate appropriate distance and conflict in relationships without surrendering your sense of what is right. **Key questions**: Should I set a boundary in this situation? Am I engaging in avoidant behaviors due to fear of conflict?

- **(Low score)** Engage in tasks for the sake of getting to know others versus for the sake of winning. Remember that victories are shallow when won at the expense of others; your accomplishments will mean very little to those around you if you've violated their trust to win. **Key questions**: Am I valuing my desire to win over the need for relational harmony? Am I being unnecessarily mistrustful of others? Will competition or cooperation serve the group more effectively in this situation?

Limiting Personal Bias

- **(High Score)** Potential blind spots: fear of conflict; fear of rejection; fear of isolation.

- **(Low Score)** Potential blind spots: fear of failure; fear of loss or losing; fear of being taken advantage of.

3e. NEUROTICISM

High Score > 4; Low Score < 2

The Neuroticism scale measures the tendency to be prone to psychological stress and to experience unpleasant emotions easily. Individuals who score high on this scale have been described as worriers who are prone to unusually high emotional vacillation. Individuals who score low on this scale have been described as able to manage stressful situations without emotional arousal and as being emotionally resilient.

Potential Strengths

- **(High Score)** Alert, mindful of surroundings, and rarely caught off guard; potentially able to thrive in chaotic energy; concerned and attentive when needs arise.

- **(Low Score)** In control, secure, stress-free.

Potential Weaknesses

- **(High Score)** May overcommit or act controllingly due to hyper-arousal or hyper-vigilance; prone to physical illness due to chronic worry and anxiety.

- **(Low Score)** May be perceived as lacking in concern or empathy; inability to respond in a timely manner; may not take serious situations with the gravity those situations warrant.

Action Points to Limit Weaknesses

- **(High Score)** Learn to distinguish the urgent from the important: Always attend to the important but think twice about the urgent. Remember that since not everyone will share your sense of urgency about most situations, it doesn't necessarily mean that they don't care as much as you or are not as invested as you. Give it the "time test" to keep perspective and to avoid catastrophizing. **Key questions**: How big of a deal will this really be in an hour? Tomorrow? Next week? Next month? Practice asking yourself and your co-leaders these questions: How will I know if I'm overreacting? What is my body telling me about my level of arousal and my need for rest? Am I the only one who perceives this situation as urgent?

- **(Low Score)** Appreciate that people who differ from you on this scale have the potential to be more responsive and attentive when needs arise. **Key questions**: Is something more required of me? Is something required of me right now? How can I help? Am I expressing an appropriate level of concern and empathy?

Limiting Personal Bias

- **(High Score)** Potential blind spots: the fear of being caught off guard; the fear of missing out.

- **(Low Score)** Potential blind spots: the fear of losing emotional control; the fear of being perceived as impulsive.

EASEL™:
3. Emotional Intelligence Domain

Jane Q. Teacher

3a. RECOGNITION OF SELF

High Score > 4; Low Score < 2

The Recognition of Self scale measures the degree to which respondents demonstrate the skill of accurately recognizing their own thoughts, feelings, strengths, and weaknesses. Key components of self-recognition include being able to recognize a wide spectrum of emotion (emotional valence) and the intensity of emotion (emotional arousal) and being able to track one's thoughts (meta-awareness). Individuals who score in the high range have been described as having the skills of being reflective, self-aware, self-confident, and insightful. Those who fall in the low range have been described as emotionally flat or reserved and might be perceived as aloof and standoffish.

The potential limitations associated with a low score on this scale include acting out emotions inappropriately (because you are not aware that you have them) and being unaware of the emotions of others (because you cannot identify them in yourself). Since much of our behavior is emotion-driven, not knowing one's emotions means not knowing why one is doing much of what one does. As Socrates famously noted, "The unexamined life is not worth living." Also, one becomes at risk for physical illness when intense emotion goes unidentified and unexpressed over time.

To develop this skill, ask trusted colleagues, friends, and families for feedback. Also, practice labeling your emotions, and practice anticipating how events might make you feel and what they might make you think. Also, practice paying attention to your body for clues about what you might be feeling—body aches, lethargy, elevated heart rate, and heart palpitations might be an indication of emotional arousal.

Key questions: Can I consistently and predictably identify my thoughts and feelings, particularly in stressful situations? Am I prone to live in my head and avoid my heart because I am uncomfortable with feelings? Did I grow up learning that emotions were okay to be experienced, or was I taught to repress and hide emotion?

3b. REGULATION OF SELF

High Score > 4; Low Score < 2

The Regulation of Self scale measures the degree to which one appropriately manages one's internal states, impulses, and resources, having identified them (see Recognition of Self scale).

Individuals who score in the high range have been described as appropriately self-controlled, mature, responsible, conscientious, adaptive, and trustworthy. Those with low scores have been described as impulsive and moody (the proverbial loose cannon).

The potential limitations associated with a low score on this scale include engaging in hurtful behaviors to vent emotion and becoming locked in intense emotion and/or behavioral patterns due to the inability to resolve emotion. Another liability is having a low tolerance for frustration, which often results in poor task performance. Unpredictable and hurtful behavior that arises from inappropriately expressed emotion sabotages relationships and creates distance between people.

To develop this skill, start by using appropriate language to express your emotion. For example, using the "I-statement" can be very helpful: "I feel [blank] about [blank] because [blank]." Part of the value of the I-statement is that it does not assign blame (e.g., "You made me feel . . ."). Also, physical exercise, walking, yoga, and sports can be an excellent way to flush out the energy associated with strong emotions, especially when those feelings result in physical symptoms like muscle tension.

Key questions: Have I linked my feelings to destructive behaviors in my life? Have I identified substitute, adaptive behaviors to express my feelings that don't harm me or others? Have I asked forgiveness from anyone that I've harmed when I've expressed my emotions inappropriately?

3c. RECOGNITION OF OTHERS

High Score > 4; Low Score < 2

The Recognition of Others scale measures the degree to which the respondent can accurately identify the thoughts and feelings of others. Individuals who score in the high range on this scale have been described as empathetic, caring, and approachable. Individuals who score low on this scale have been described as emotionally aloof, detached, and uncaring.

A primary potential liability associated with a low score on this scale is relational isolation. When people that depend on me do not feel seen, heard, or known by me (because I lack the empathy to connect with them), they tend to develop a trust deficit. Individuals who lack empathy have difficulty engaging in nurturing, supportive behaviors toward those around them, leaving others around them to assume that they are on their own.

To develop this skill, practice being curious about others and getting to know their story; get to know people who are not like you culturally, demographically, religiously, politically, or generationally. Practice asking open-ended questions, such as "How are you feeling today?" or "How was your weekend?" or "Is there anything I can do to help you today?"

Key questions: Have I gone out of my way to know more about the people I work with most? Have I made it a point to understand the thoughts, feelings, and struggles of those around me? What have I done to express to those around me my appreciation for who they are and what they do?

3d. REGULATION OF OTHERS

High Score > 4; Low Score < 2

The Regulation of Others scale measures the capacity to lead others in effective dyadic or group dynamics based on the personal and collective thoughts and feelings that bear upon a given situation. Individuals who score high on this scale have been described as excellent leaders, socially adept, interpersonally accessible, and attuned to group dynamics. Individuals who score low have been described as ineffective leaders, passive, disengaged, and out of touch with group needs and dynamics.

In any leadership role, the potential liabilities associated with a low score on this scale include frequent miscommunication with others due to poor communication skills, and the growth of a toxic and dysfunctional culture due to my inability to effectively resolve conflict.

To develop this skill, practice effective interpersonal skills. For example, be a good listener by asking good questions and by focusing on what the person is saying rather than what you'd like to say next. Also practice good non-verbal skills, such as maintaining good eye contact when someone is speaking, maintaining a good proximity to the speaker, and making appropriate facial expressions. Additionally, practice good conflict resolution skills by staying alert and calm when conflict is present between you and another, or when you are mediating conflict between two others. Encourage and practice forgiveness and compromise to move toward effective resolution.

Key questions: Have I practiced good listening skills? Do I avoid having difficult conversations and, in so doing, sustain conflict or delay healthy resolution?

EASEL™:
4. Stress Management Domain

Jane Q. Teacher

4a. Stress Resilience

High Score > 4; Low Score < 2

The Stress Resilience scale measures the individual's overall vulnerability to stress. The three Stress Resilience subscales are the Optimism, Tolerance, and Flexibility scale. If you scored in the low range on the Stress Resilience Total scale, you are highly vulnerable to stress. Since stress is energy we produce when we wonder whether we can deal effectively with a threatening or challenging situation, a low Stress Resilience Total score means that you are more at risk for hypertension and a host of other physical symptoms that arise due to chronic stress. If you scored in the high range, you are more resilient to stress, meaning you can adaptively tolerate more stress than the average person. See the Adaptive Engaging and Adaptive Disengaging summaries for strategies to effectively manage stress.

4b. ADAPTIVE ENGAGING

High Score > 4; Low Score < 2

The Capacity for Adaptive Engaging scale measures the individual's innate propensity to access stress energy as a fuel source to engage (i.e., the "fight" in the often-referenced fight-or-flight fear response) in ways that lead to favorable outcomes for self and others. Individuals who score high have been described as task oriented and able to get things done. Those who score low have been described as neglecting responsibilities and potentially maladaptively passive.

The stress management strategies that are most often associated with adaptive engaging include the following:

- **Anticipate.** Think ahead to the people, places, times, and events that will challenge you. Be prepared to respond to them ahead of time so that when the stressors arise, you will not be caught off guard.

- **Get connected.** Consider the source of your stress and ask yourself whether you know anyone who has walked through this before. While the event may be stressful to you, there is a good chance that you know someone who has experienced the issue before, and they may have good advice for you about how to successfully navigate it. Even if you don't know anyone who can offer you guidance or coaching, there is often tremendous benefit in simply having a listening ear—someone who can empathize with you and offer you comfort.

- **Exercise.** As we noted in the Regulation of Self scale, finding some type of physical activity to release our stress energy can be a very adaptive, healthy outlet. After a good workout or physical activity, we will be more ready to initiate and sustain sleep rather than lying in bed with too much energy and racing thoughts.

- **Set boundaries.** As noted in the action points of the Neuroticism scale, learning to differentiate the urgent from the important is an essential skill if one wishes to set good boundaries. We are managing stress effectively when we set healthy boundaries in relationships, in work, and even in play.

When we access the energy that stress produces to engage the strategies listed here, we grow our adaptive psychological coping muscles using the fight skill set. However, we can also engage in ways that are hurtful and not helpful. For example, attacking, blaming, and criticizing others may relieve some of our stress in the moment, but those kinds of engaging strategies are, in fact, maladaptive and relationally damaging.

4c. ADAPTIVE DISENGAGING

High Score > 4; Low Score < 2

The Capacity for Adaptive Disengaging scale measures the individual's innate ability to access stress energy as a fuel source to avoid (i.e., the "flight" in the fight-or-flight fear response) in ways that lead to favorable outcomes for self and others. Individuals who score high have been described as reflective and considerate. Individuals who score in the low range have been described as potentially lacking in insight and perspective.

The stress management strategies that are most often associated with adaptive disengaging include the following:

- **Practice self-observation.** It's a difficult question to face, but ask yourself: What might I be doing to contribute to the problem? How might at least some portion of my stress be rooted in my own insecurity or blind spot? How can I approach this stressful situation as an opportunity to learn more about myself and my own weaknesses?

- **Keep perspective.** This goes back to the time test referenced in the Neuroticism scale (the Neuroticism scale is highly correlated with the Stress Management scales). Practice asking yourself these questions: How big of a deal will this really be in an hour? Tomorrow? Next week? Next month? Those questions help us keep the big picture in mind. Also, the following questions can be helpful to keep perspective: How will I know if I'm overreacting? What is my body telling me about my level of arousal and my need for rest? Am I the only one who perceives this situation as urgent?

When we tap into the energy produced by stress to avoid using the strategies listed above, we utilize a second skill set—the flight skill set—to grow our adaptive psychological coping muscles. However, we can also avoid in ways that are hurtful and not helpful. For example, if I avoid by being apathetic, rationalizing my faults and failures, or denying my contribution to the problems, that kind of disengagement may help me sleep at night, but it will be relationally damaging.

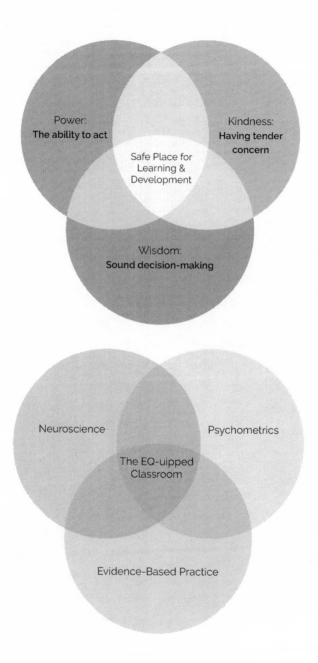

Index

*Page references to figures are indicated by *f*'s.

A

acknowledging and apologizing, role in
  conflict resolution, 160–61
actuarial validity, 39–40
Adler, Alfred, 121
aggressive communication style, 151–52
Agreeableness personality trait, 69–70,
  72*f*–73*f*
  aggressive communication style and,
    152
  Agreeableness scale (EASEL), 224–26
  empathy and, 133
  passive communication style and, 151
  regulating weakness associated with,
    99–101
amygdala, 62, 89
Aristotle, iii
assertive communication style, 153–55
autonomic nervous system, 62

B

Baldwin, James, 167
Behavioral Intervention Plan. *See* BIP
behavior management
  of off-task behavior, 174–79
  stick-and-carrot strategy, 195–96
  teaching self-awareness to students,
    189–92

Big 5 Model of personality, 7–8, 65–74.
  *See also names of specific personality
  traits*
Binet, Alfred, 13
Binet-Simon Measuring Scale for Intelligence, 32–33
BIP (Behavioral Intervention Plan),
  110–14
  defined, 110–11
  identifying feelings, 111
  linking feelings with behavior, 111–13
  for students, 179–82
  substituting behavior, 113–14
  for teachers, 182–84
Brigham, Carl, 36
Bryson, Tina Payne, 191

C

Capacity for Adaptive Disengaging scale,
  EASEL, 236–38
Capacity for Adaptive Engaging scale,
  EASEL, 235–36
Carroll, John B., 34
CASEL (Collaborative for Academic,
  Social, and Emotional Learning),
  13, 41
Cattell, Raymond B., 34

Charcot, Jean-Martin, 31
CHC (Cattell-Horn-Carroll) theory, 34–35
Choice Theory (Glasser), 188
clinical validity, 40
Collaborative for Academic, Social, and Emotional Learning (CASEL), 13, 41
communication
  aggressive communication style, 151–52
  assertive communication style, 153–55
  I-statement, 113, 160
  listening skills, 128–30, 143
  non-verbal communication, 131–32, 143
  paraverbal communication, 130–31, 143
  passive-aggressive communication style, 153
  passive communication style, 150–51
conflict resolution, 155–63, 164
  general discussion, 155–58
  guiding students through, 185
  healthy practices, 159–63
    acknowledging and apologizing for role in conflict, 160–61, 163*f*
    clarifying reason for conflict, 159–60, 163*f*
    cool-down/calm space, 159, 163*f*
    forgiving, 161, 163*f*
    identifying facts, 160, 163*f*
    identifying feelings, 160, 163*f*
    identifying patterns, 160, 163*f*
    involving third party if necessary, 161–62, 163*f*
    negotiating, 161, 163*f*
  maladaptive responses, 158–59
  trust and, 158
Conscientiousness personality trait, 66–67, 72*f*–73*f*
  aggressive communication style and, 152
  Conscientiousness scale (EASEL), 220–22
  empathy and, 133
  regulating weakness associated with, 96–98
contingent communication, 129
cooperative learning, 186

crystallized intelligence, 34–35

D

decision-making. *See* responsible decision-making
Deming, W. Edwards, 40
Different Drum, The (Peck), 87–88
Dozier, James Lee, 17–20
Durlak, Joseph, 28

E

EASEL (Educator Assessment of Social and Emotional Learning)
  Big 5 Model of personality, 7–8, 65–74
  Emotional Intelligence Domain, 229–33
    Recognition of Others scale, 133, 232
    Recognition of Self scale, 63, 229–30
    Regulation of Others scale, 233
    Regulation of Self scale, 230–31
  Personality Domain, 218–28
    Agreeableness scale, 224–26
    Conscientiousness scale, 220–22
    Extraversion scale, 222–24
    Neuroticism scale, 226–28
    Openness to Experience scale, 218–20
  role in EQ-uipped Classroom curriculum, 5
  sample report, 211–13
  Social Desirability scale, 217
  Stress Management Domain, 234–38
    Capacity for Adaptive Disengaging scale, 236–38
    Capacity for Adaptive Engaging scale, 235–36
    Stress Resilience scale, 234
elementary school, learning self-awareness in, 190–91
emotional hygiene, 27
emotional intelligence. *See* EQ
Emotional Intelligence Domain, EASEL, 229–33
  Recognition of Others scale, 232
  Recognition of Self scale, 229–30
  Regulation of Others scale, 233

Regulation of Self scale, 230–31
Emotional Intelligence (Goleman), 41
emotions, 61–64
    dangers of avoiding, 93–94
    identifying in order to resolve conflict,
        160
    self-awareness, 61–64
    self-regulation, 89–94, 119
    social awareness, 128–32
        listening skills, 128–30
        non-verbal communication, 131–32
        paraverbal communication, 130–31
    of students
        ignoring, 174–76
        inhibiting, 176
        invalidating, 177
        inviting, 177–79
empathy. *See also* social awareness
    importance of, 143
    sympathy versus, 128
    trust and, 133–34
EQ (emotional intelligence). *See also* SEL
    measuring, 37–42
    quality of life and, 25–29
    sample test, 46–50
EQ-uipped classroom, 167
    social contract, 187–88, 187*f*
    student awareness of others, 185
    student regulation of others, 186–88
    student self-awareness, 174–79, 189
    student self-regulation, 179–82
    teacher self-awareness and self-regula-
        tion, 182–84
    VUCA, 172–74
ethics
    measuring EQ, 37
    measuring IQ, 29–37
etiquette, 146–49, 164
external storms. *See* stress
Extraversion personality trait, 68–69,
    72*f*–73*f*
    empathy and, 133
    Extraversion scale (EASEL), 222–24
    regulating weakness associated with,
        98–99
eye contact
    aggressive communication style, 152
    assertive communication style, 154

non-verbal communication, 131
passive communication style, 151

F

facial expressions, non-verbal communi-
    cation, 131
fight-or-flight response, 62, 74–75, 89,
    109*f*
fluid intelligence, 34
forgiveness, role in conflict resolution, 161
Frames of Mind (Gardner), 38–39

G

Gandhi, Mahatma, 193
Garcia, Mike, 1–4
gardening metaphor, for SEL, 195
Gardner, Howard, 13, 38–40
George Washington University Social
    Intelligence Test, 38
Glasser, William, 188
Goddard, Henry, 32–33
Goleman, Daniel, 13, 41, 145

H

heart smarts. *See also* SEL
    defined, 3–4
high school, learning self-awareness in,
    191–92
high-table dinner event, 147–49
Horn, John L., 34
Hunt, Thelma, 38, 42
hypnotism (subconscious automatism), 31

I

IDEA (Individuals with Disabilities
    Education Act), 11–12
ignoring emotions, 174–76
individuating, 193–94
Ingham, Harrison, 60
inhibiting emotions, 176
insecurities, 59–60. *See also* self-awareness

Inside Out (movie), 191
intelligence quotient (IQ), 29–37, 42–46
internal climate. *See* personality types;
  self-awareness
introverts, 222
invalidating emotions, 177
inviting emotions, 177–79
IQ (intelligence quotient), 29–37, 42–46
I-statement, 113, 160

J

Johari Window, 60–61, 60*f*
Jung, Carl, 57

K

kidnapping of General Dozier, 17–20

L

learning disabilities
  diagnosing with discrepancy model,
    11–12
  testing for, 35–36
Life Givers, 26*f*, 52–53
Life Suckers, 26*f*, 52–53
listening skills, 128–30, 143
Locke, John, 186
Luft, Joseph, 60

M

maladaptive responses, conflict resolution,
  158–59
Mann, Horace, 29
Mayer, John, 40–41
Mayer-Solovey-Caruso Emotional Intelligence Test, 41
McCartney, Paul, 59
mental age, defined, 32
mental health. *See also* SEL
  effect of chaos on, 9
  role of SEL in, 24

middle school, learning self-awareness
  in, 191
Morton, Samuel, 29–31
multiple intelligences theory, 39–40
Mya, adoption of, 124–25

N

negotiating conflict resolution, 161
Neuroticism personality trait, 70–71,
  72*f*–73*f*, 74
  Neuroticism scale (EASEL), 226–28
  regulating weakness associated with,
    101–2
non-contingent communication, 129
non-verbal communication, 131–32, 143

O

off-task behavior, of students, 174–79
open-ended questions, 132
Openness to experience personality trait,
  65–66, 72*f*–73*f*
  Openness to experience scale (EASEL),
    218–20
  regulating weakness associated with,
    94–96

P

parasympathetic nervous system, 62
paraverbal communication, 130–31, 143
passive-aggressive communication style,
  153
passive communication style, 150–51
patterns, conflict, 160
Peck, M. Scott, 87–88
Personality Domain, EASEL, 218–28
  Agreeableness scale, 224–26
  Conscientiousness scale, 220–22
  Extraversion scale, 222–24
  Neuroticism scale, 226–28
  Openness to Experience scale, 218–20

personality types. *See also names of specific personality types*
Agreeableness
  self-awareness and, 69–70
  self-regulation and, 99–101
Conscientiousness
  self-awareness and, 66–67
  self-regulation and, 96–98
Extraversion
  self-awareness and, 68–69
  self-regulation and, 98–99
Neuroticism
  self-awareness and, 70–71, 74
  self-regulation and, 101–2
Openness to experience
  self-awareness and, 65–66
  self-regulation and, 94–96
overview, 83, 119
self-awareness and, 64–74
social awareness and, 132–34
Peterson, Jordan, 7–10, 40
phrenology, 29–31
Power of a Teacher, The (Saenz), 4
pre-school, learning self-awareness in, 189–90
psychological exposure, 59–60, 83
psychometric assessments, 31–37
  Binet-Simon Measuring Scale for Intelligence, 32–33
  CHC theory, 34–35
  controversy about, 36–37
  learning disabilities, 35–36
  role of Alfred Binet in developing, 31–32
  role of Theodore Simon in developing, 31–32
  Stanford-Binet Intelligence Test, 33
  Wechsler Adult Intelligence Scale, 34
  Wechsler Intelligence Scale for Children, 34
psychomotor agitation, non-verbal communication, 131

Q

quality of life, EQ and, 25–29

R

Recognition of Others scale, EASEL, 133, 232
Recognition of Self scale, EASEL, 63, 229–30
Red Brigades, 18
Regulation of Others scale, EASEL, 233
Regulation of Self scale, EASEL, 230–31
relational isolation, 133–34
relationship skills
  communication styles, 150–55, 164
    aggressive, 151–52
    assertive, 153–55
    passive, 150–51
    passive-aggressive, 153
  conflict resolution, 155–63, 164
    general discussion, 155–58
    healthy practices, 159–63
    maladaptive responses, 158–59
    trust and, 158–59
  defined, 14, 42
  etiquette versus, 146–49, 164
  of General Dozier during kidnapping, 19–20
  overview, 145–46
  social contracts, 186–88
Relationships That Work (Saenz), 4
repressing emotions, 77, 150–51, 176
responsible decision-making, 197
  defined, 42
  of General Dozier during kidnapping, 20
  of Mr. Seaman during school shooting, 22–23
rest-and-digest response, 62, 89
Rogers, Fred, 87

S

Salovey, Peter, 40–41
school safety, inside-out approach to, 3–4
school shootings
  US Secret Service statistics for, 173
  West Noblesville Middle School, 20–23
Seaman, Jason, 20–23

Seigel, Daniel J., 191
self-awareness
  author's journey into, 79–83
  Biblical account of Adam and Eve,
    57–59
  case example, 76–79
  defined, 41, 83
  EASEL Big 5 Personality Traits,
    72f–73f
  emotions, 61–64, 75f
  fear of psychological exposure, 59–60
  of General Dozier during kidnapping,
    19
  Johari Window, 60–61, 60f
  of Mr. Seaman during school shooting,
    22–23
  of personality, 64–74, 75f
    Agreeableness, 69–70
    Big 5 Model, 65
    Conscientiousness, 66–67
    Extraversion, 68–69
    Neuroticism, 70–71, 74
    Openness to experience, 65–66
  stress, 74–75, 75f
    physical indications of, 74–75
    sympathetic nervous system and, 74
  of teachers, 182–84
  teaching to students, 174–79, 189
self-care, teachers, 184
self-regulation
  author's journey into, 115–19
  case example, 110–15
  defined, 41–42
  emotions, 89–94
  of General Dozier during kidnapping,
    19
  of Mr. Seaman during school shooting,
    22–23
  overview, 87–89
  of personality, 94–103
    Agreeableness, 99–101
    Conscientious, 96–98
    Extraversion, 98–99
    Neuroticism, 101–2
    Openness to experience, 94–96
  stress, 103–9
  of students, 179–82

of teachers, 182–84
SEL (Social and Emotional Learn-
    ing). See also names of specific SEL
    components
  application in daily life, 23–29
  author's early research in, 1
  EQ-uipped Classroom, 167
    social contract, 187–88, 187f
    student awareness of others, 185
    student regulation of others, 186–88
    student self-awareness, 174–79, 189
    student self-regulation, 179–82
    teacher self-awareness and self-regula-
      tion, 182–84
    VUCA, 172–74
  interventions, 52–53
  Life Givers versus Life Suckers, 23–29,
    26f
  personal relevance to author, 6
  questioning validity of, 9–11
  relationship between traumatic stress
    and
    kidnapping case example, 17–20
    school shooting case example, 20–23
  responsible decision-making, 42
  self-awareness, 41
  self-regulation, 41–42
  social skills, 14, 42
  teaching, 50–54
Shattered Mind, The (Gardner), 39
Simon, Theodore, 31–32
Social and Emotional Learning. See SEL
social awareness
  author's journey into, 138–42
  case example, 134–37
  defined, 42
  developing, 14
  of General Dozier during kidnapping,
    19
  importance of, 125–28, 143
  listening skills, 143
  of Mr. Seaman during school shooting,
    22–23
  non-verbal communication, 143
  of others' emotions, 128–32
    listening skills, 128–30
    non-verbal communication, 131–32

paraverbal communication, 130–31
of others' personalities, 132–34, 143
paraverbal communication, 143
of students, 185
social contract, 186–88, 187*f*, 189
Social Desirability scale, EASEL, 217
social skills
  communication styles, 150–55, 164
    aggressive, 151–52
    assertive, 153–55
    passive, 150–51
    passive-aggressive, 153
  conflict resolution, 155–63, 164
    general discussion, 155–58
    healthy practices, 159–63
    maladaptive responses, 158–59
    trust and, 158–59
  defined, 14, 42
  etiquette versus, 146–49, 164
  of General Dozier during kidnapping,
    19–20
  overview, 145–46
  social contracts, 186–88
Socrates, 63
Spearman, Charles, 33
speed of speech, paraverbal communica-
    tion, 130–31
spirituality, personality theory and, 8–9
Stanford-Binet Intelligence Test, 33
stick-and-carrot strategy, behavior man-
    agement, 195–96
stigma, of intellectual disability nomen-
    clature, 32–33
stress
  relationship between SEL and
    kidnapping case example, 17–20
    school shooting case example, 20–23
  self-awareness and, 74–75
    physical indications of, 74–75
    sympathetic nervous system and, 74
  self-regulation and, 103–9, 119
    anticipating stressors, 106
    connecting with others, 106
    EASEL Capacity for Adaptive Engag-
      ing scale, 106–8
    exercise, 107

helpful stress management strategies,
    109*f*
hurtful stress management strategies,
    109*f*
keeping perspective, 108
self-observation, 108
setting boundaries, 107
Stress Management Domain, EASEL,
    234–38
  Capacity for Adaptive Disengaging
    scale, 236–38
  Capacity for Adaptive Engaging scale,
    235–36
  Stress Resilience scale, 234
Strudwick, Canon Vincent, 147
students
  awareness of others, 185
  learning self-awareness, 174–79
    in high school, 191–92
    ignoring emotions, 174–76
    inhibiting emotions, 176
    invalidating emotions, 177
    inviting emotions, 177–79
    in lower elementary, 190
    in middle school, 191
    in pre-school, 189–90
    in upper elementary, 190–91
  regulation of others, 186–88
  self-regulation, 179–82
subconscious automatism (hypnotism), 31
sympathetic nervous system, 62, 74
sympathy, defined, 128

T

teachers
  importance of self-care, 184
  self-awareness, 182–84
  self-regulation, 182–84
  teaching self-awareness to students,
    189–92
    high school, 191–92
    ignoring students' emotions, 174–76
    inhibiting students' emotions, 176
    invalidating students' emotions, 177
    inviting students' emotions, 177–79

lower elementary, 190
middle school, 191
pre-school, 189–90
upper elementary, 190–91
Terman, Lewis, 32–33, 36–37
therapist/client relationship, 146
third party involvement, in conflict reso-
    lution, 161–62
Thorndike, Edward, 37–38, 42
360 assessment, 217
tone, paraverbal communication, 130
toxic practices, conflict resolution, 158–59
traumatic stress
    kidnapping case example, 17–20
    school shooting case example, 20–23
trust
    conflict resolution and, 158–59
    empathy and, 133–34

V

validity
    actuarial, 39–40
    clinical, 40
volume, paraverbal communication, 130
VUCA (volatility, uncertainty, complexity,
    and ambiguity) concept, 172–74
vulnerability (psychological exposure),
    59–60, 83

W

Webb-Hasan, Gwen, 5
Wechsler Adult Intelligence Scale, 34
Wechsler, David, 34, 38
Wechsler Intelligence Scale for Children,
    34
Whole-Brain Child, The (Seigel and
    Bryson), 191

Y

Yoon, Myeongsun, 5

Acknowledgments

Thank you, Texas Elementary Principals and Supervisors Association, for the ongoing privilege of presenting our research and clinical work at the TEPSA Summer Conference and other TEPSA events over the years. Your commitment to leaders in education inspires me to do my best work. Harley Eckhart, Joni Carlson, Belinda Neal, Mark Terry, and Trae Kendrick—you all (and the rest!) are gold.

In a similar vein, I must thank the Texas Association of Secondary School Principals for the honor of presenting my work at the TASSP Summer Workshop and other TASSP events over the years. Again, knowing your passion to empower leaders in education compels me as a psychologist to empower and equip all those who are leading and serving on campuses across Texas. Archie McAffee, Cindy Jackson, Emily Mikolaitis, and Billy Pringle, you all have rock star status in my book.

Amy Jensen, thank you for your work polishing the manuscript. You were exactly what the rough manuscript needed, and your insights as a writer and educator brought tremendous value to the process and the final product.

Thank you, Greenleaf Book Group. Absolutely top notch.

Daniel Sandoval, Daniel Peterson, and the rest of the team, you have, with mindful skill and care, transformed a manuscript into a book that I am proud to release.

Thank you, Trish Stevens and the team at Ascot Media Group, for your efforts to let the nation know that a book has been released that can empower educators to achieve increased professional performance and sustainability, and empower students to deeper and richer interpersonal relationships and higher academic achievement.

Tess Lowe and the Second Melody team, thank you for helping me think through what emotional intelligence means for someone who is not a psychologist, what Applied EQ Group should look like, and how to present our offerings to the marketplace.

Thank you, Jeremy Dew, L.P.C.-S., for excelling in your role as clinical director at The Oakwood Collaborative and at the Roots clinic. Thanks also to the rest of our clinical team who serve the children, adults, families, and couples in the Brazos Valley: Robert Larson, Ph.D., Sophia Tani, Ph.D., Erin Sandoval, Ph.D., James Deegear, Ph.D., Nicole Hale, Ph.D., Jackie Womack, L.M.F.T., Lauri Baker-Brown, L.P.C., Jared Meyer, L.P.C.-I., Cameron House, L.P.C., Evelyn Ramos, L.P.C., and Elizabeth Eaton, L.P.C.-S.

Taylor Arnett, you have proven to be absolutely stellar in your ability to successfully manage our clinic. I'm excited about your starting a graduate program in counseling this fall, and I have no doubt that you will become an in-demand therapist sooner than you realize. Your future is bright, and we are delighted for every moment we get to be a part of it.

This book and the associated assessment—the Educator Assessment of Social and Emotional Learning (EASEL)—would be less than what they are now without the contributions of two faculty in the College of Education at Texas A&M University. First, Myeongsun Yoon, Ph.D., you and your team's psychometric analysis of the EASEL's data has provided exactly what we need to feel good about using it as a tool with the clients we coach in professional development. Thank you for your partnership. Also, Gwen Webb-Hasan, Ph.D., I am deeply grateful to you for the invitations to have presented material from this book and *The Power of a Teacher* with your graduate students over the past semesters; I appreciate the work you are doing to remind us how empathy and perspective-taking will reduce our bias against populations whose voice is not yet readily heard.

Thank you, Alisa, Mya, Isaiah, and Andrew. Fatherhood persistently re-invites a man to know and regulate himself, and to know and interact with the world around him. Each of you are growing in your capacities to do the same, and as you do so, you can be confident that you will become the best versions of yourselves, living the best life you can possibly live. I love you.

Kim, it's been a total of twenty-eight years now: two of dating, two of engagement, and twenty-four of marriage. Our journey together has been one of learning into, though, and out of each new season: We learn more about ourselves, we learn how to regulate what we find, we learn about each other, and we learn how to (re)connect with what we find in each other. It's certainly not always been easy work, but aren't we immeasurably richer for it? With each passing season, aren't we continually becoming the best version of us? I think Marlene was right: We are blessed that we consider each other a best friend—each a part of the other's inner circle. I love you.

About the Author

Dr. Adam L. Saenz earned his Ph.D. in School Psychology from Texas A&M University as a United States Department of Education doctoral fellow. He completed his predoctoral clinical training under a fellowship appointment to Harvard Medical School, and he has a postdoctorate in clinical psychology from the Alpert Medical School of Brown University. Dr. Saenz also earned a Doctorate of Ministry in Pastoral Counseling from Graduate Theological Foundation with residency at Christ Church college of Oxford University.

Dr. Saenz is the author of the best-selling book, *The Power of a Teacher*. He currently serves as the Executive Director of the Oakwood Collaborative, a counseling and assessment clinic he founded in 2003, and he consults with school systems internationally in the areas of emotional intelligence, self-care, and the dynamics of relationship-based learning. In addition to his clinical work, Dr. Saenz serves as a high school track and field coach. He is a member of the Association for Applied Sports Psychology, and he is a lifetime member of the Texas Track and Field Coaches Association.

Dr. Saenz and his wife, Kim, have been married twenty-three years, and they have four children: Alisa, Mya, Isaiah, and Andrew.

in the USA
ppell, TX
ember 2023

00155